Viola

The Magic of Music Theory

Book 1

Kristin Campbell

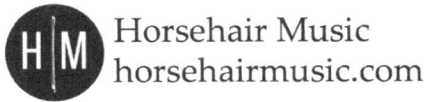

Horsehair Music
horsehairmusic.com

Book 1 Violin: ISBN 978-1-959514-15-2; Library of Congress Number: 2025916302
Book 1 Viola: ISBN 978-1-959514-18-3; Library of Congress Number: 2025916303
Book 1 Cello: ISBN 978-1-959514-16-9 Library of Congress Number: 2025916304

This book is dedicated to Laura Crawford and Charles Regauer, directors of the Centenary Suzuki School in Shreveport, Louisiana. Thank you for welcoming me into your Suzuki family and giving me a platform to teach theory to string students.

Special thanks to Ruth Coleman for her editorial help. Thanks to all the students who have tested out these pages and activities.

Graphics:
Cover Design: Christiana Hudson and Kristin Campbell
Hand image by www.vectorportal.com
String instruments, fingerboard, bow, color by beat images by Kristin Campbell
Haydn Graphic Licensed from Florida Center for Instructional Technology
All other images from www.freesvg.com

To the student:

Welcome to the Magic of Music Theory! Did you know that when you write things on paper it helps you remember them? This book is to help you remember things that you have learned in your lesson about your viola, and you learn how to read and write music. If you need help you can always ask your practice partner, or your teacher will help. When you finish this book, you will know and understand more about your viola and playing music. It's like magic, the magic of music theory!

To the practice partner:

You are the viola hero. Practicing isn't always fun, and it's not always easy. But in this journey of learning to play the viola, you get to walk alongside a child and give them the gift of music that will last for a lifetime.

Depending on age and reading ability, you may need to assist the student with their assignments. You can learn along with them. Don't be afraid to help and lead the student to the answer. Your child may not grasp it the first time. That's ok! You will find a lot of review built in through out the book. With repetition and review they will begin to understand and remember. This is the learning process.

Keep theory time short! You can choose to do the lesson at the end of one practice session, or you could choose do a little bit each day. It's up to you. Ask your teacher their preference on the "What Do You Hear?" pages. You can complete them in the lesson, access videos online or download free mp3 tracks. The answers are given at the end of each question on the video/track, so that the student gets immediate feedback in the learning process. Enjoy the magic of learning music theory!

To the teacher:

I created this series because I wanted to engage a different part of students' thinking in the music learning process. The worksheets also gave me data for how they were processing and understanding. Many good theory curriculums approach the subject from a keyboard perspective. This makes it hard for young students who are not taking keyboard lessons. I found I was using valuable lesson time to explain theory pages. I needed something they could do at home, apply to their violin playing, and that only required a short explanation in the lesson. The parent could also assist if needed.

I am a Suzuki teacher. So, my approach to teaching is that students first learn to play the instrument, then learn to read, then learn to write/notate. Their note reading and writing (theory) level will be behind their playing level. I would encourage teachers to put students in a theory level below the note reading level. Students gain confidence when the workbook reinforces concepts that they already know and can execute on the instrument. You will find that the concepts are approached first from the music alphabet, then moved onto the fingerboard, and finally moved onto the staff.

The aural skills pages are designed to teach rhythmic and melodic dictation in small steps. The "What Do You Hear?" pages can be done in the lesson, through online videos, or free mp3 tracks. (Visit www.horsehairmusic.com to download tracks.) Suggested listening and recordings are linked to online videos, but feel free to select a different recording or artist to share with your students. I hope these workbooks help your studio and your students to thrive and flourish in their musical journeys.

The Magic of Music Theory Series Guide

Use this chart to help find the level that is right for your student.

Ages 6 & up Repertoire Book 1	Ages 7 & up Repertoire Book 2	Ages 7 & up Repertoire Late Book 2 & up	Ages 8 & up Repertoire Book 3 & up
Magic of Music Theory: Primer	**Magic of Music Theory: Book 1**	**Magic of Music Theory: Book 2**	**Magic of Music Theory: Book 3**
• Student has begun reading in school. • Student is ready or has begun note reading. • Student can write all letters of English alphabet. • Introduces staff notes for 2 upper strings. • After completion move to Book 1.	• Student is reading chapter books in school. • Student knows the letter names for A and D string fingerboard notes. • Student can read A and D String staff notes well. • Student needs reinforcing of lower string staff reading. • Student has played 1 octave scale beginning on an open string and is ready to learn to read and write major scale pattern. • Student understand down and up bow concept. • After completion move to Book 2.	• Student can read all staff notes in first position. • Understand how to play "high" and "low" fingers. Ready to learn how to write and draw chromatic staff pitches. • Has played slurs and hooked bows ready to learn to write bowing in score. • Has played 1 octave scales of C, G, D, A. • Confident in reading note values. • After completion move to Book 3.	• Student easily read staff notes in first position in alto clef. Ready to learn reading in another clef. • Can play and read eighth notes, sixteenth notes and triplets. Ready to learn writing these note values in simple and compound meters. • Confident in understanding and counting simple meter. Ready to learn compound meter. • Can play 1 octave scales in first position. Ready to learn writing key signatures. • Understand basic bow markings – down, up, slur, staccato, hooked bow.

Table of Contents

The Magic of Music Theory Book 1 - © 2025 Horsehair Music. Photocopying prohibited.

Lesson 1

Pitch is the sound of each note. We identify pitches using the first seven letters of the English alphabet.

1. To see the music alphabet, write one letter of the alphabet in each octagon. Once you get to G, start over at the letter A.

2. Read the music alphabet out loud. Notice that once you get to G, you start over at the letter A and repeat the 7 letters.

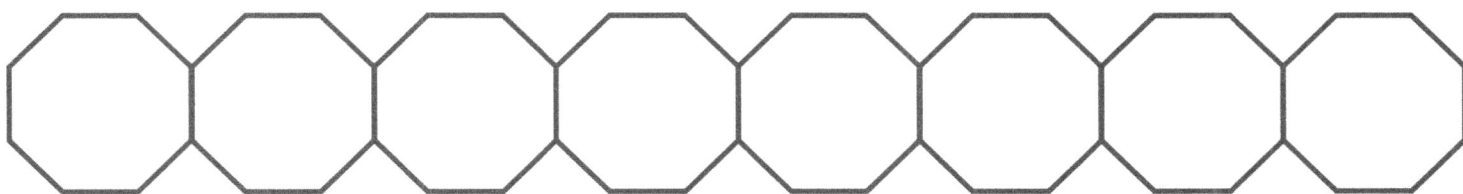

A B C D E F G A B C D E F G

3. Fill in the missing music alphabet ladders. Begin at the bottom and go up!

B		F	
	C		
G			
	A	C	E
			D
D			C
	E	G	
B		F	
A	C		G

Each finger on the left hand has a number. The number in the circle shows the line where each finger lands on the fingerboard.

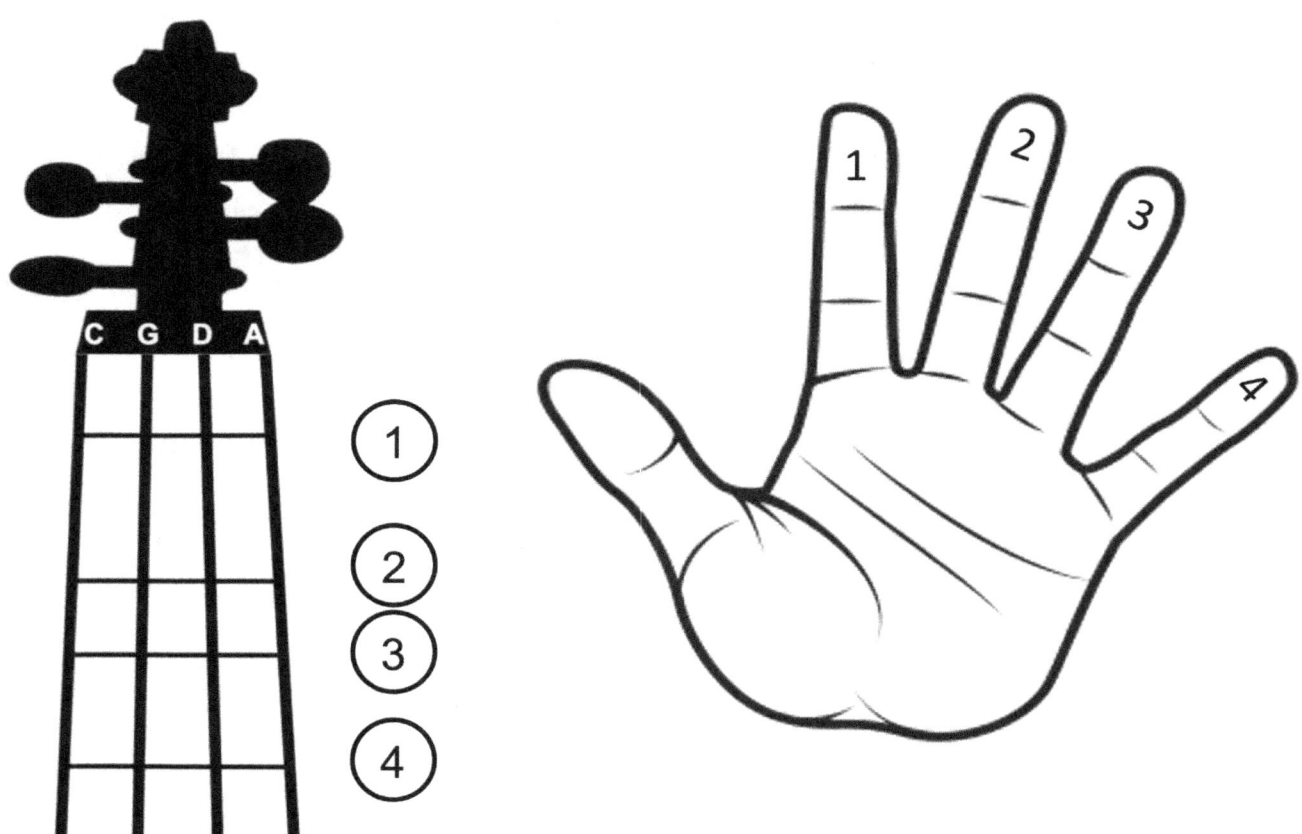

4. On the hand below write the finger number on each finger.
5. Write the finger number in the circle next to the correct line.
6. Draw a line matching the finger to the number on the fingerboard.

Lesson 2

The violin, viola, cello, and bass are members of the **string family**. The **violin** is the smallest member and plays the highest notes. The **viola** [vee-o-luh] is a little bigger than the violin and plays 5 notes lower than the violin. The **cello** [chel-oh] sounds lower than both the violin and viola. Cellists sit down and rest the instrument between their knees to play. The **double bass** is the largest member of the string family and plays the lowest notes. Sometimes it is called bass (like *base*ball) for short.

Chamber music is when a small group of people play together. Chamber music was originally written to be performed in small settings, like homes, for family and friends rather than for large audiences in theaters or churches. When 2 people play music together it is called a **duet** [doo-et]. When 3 people play together it is called a **trio** [tree-oh]. When 4 people play together it is called a **quartet** [core-tet]. Most often a **string quartet** has 2 violins, 1 viola, and 1 cello. The violinist who plays the melody is called the **first violin** or Violin 1. The violinist who plays the harmony is called the **second violin,** or Violin 2. But the first violin doesn't always have the melody, sometimes a composer will pass the melody to the other instruments in the quartet. Since there is no conductor for chamber music, a string quartet sits close together in a semi-circle. This helps them to play together because they can hear and see each other.

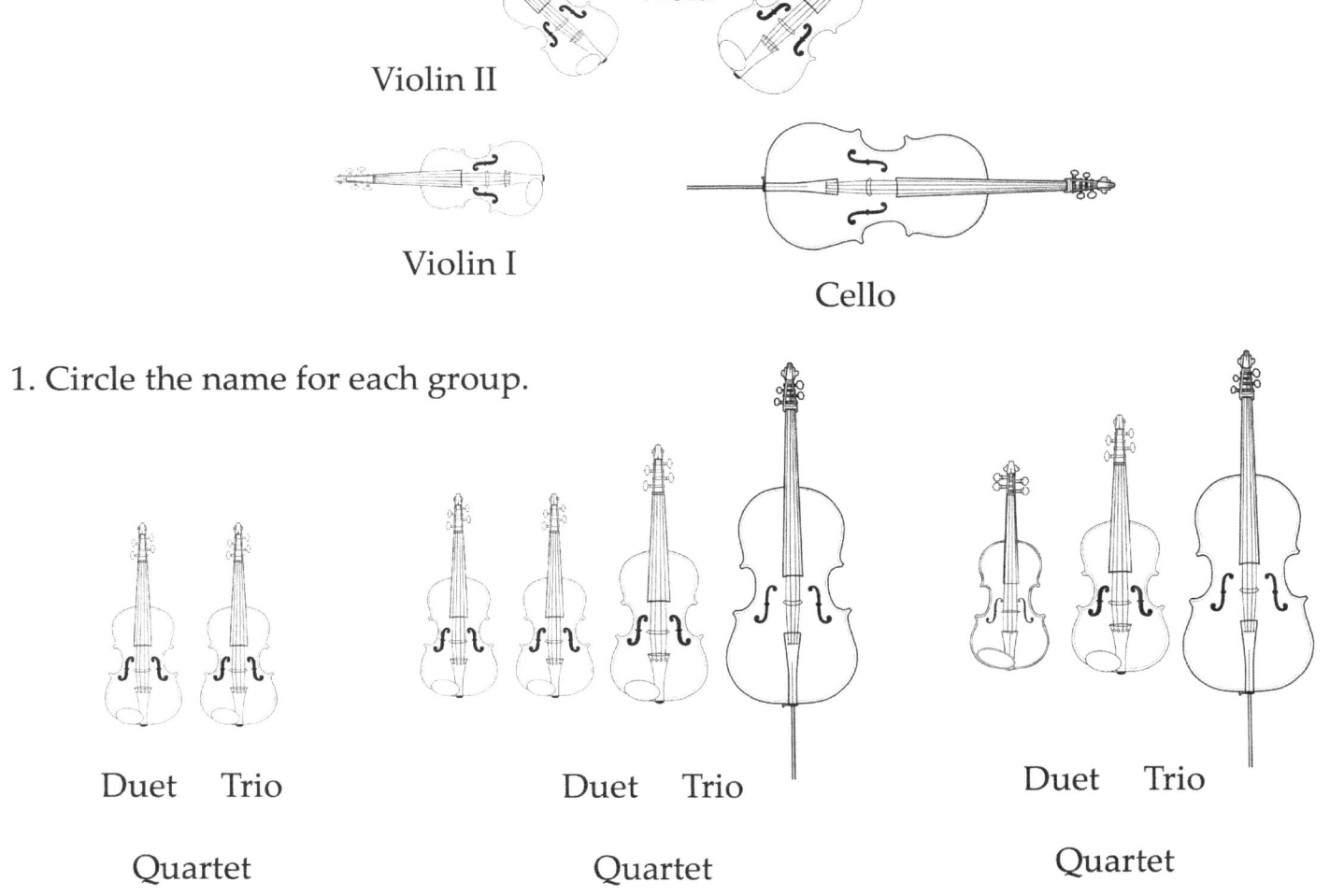

1. Circle the name for each group.

Duet   Trio

Quartet

Duet   Trio

Quartet

Duet   Trio

Quartet

Fingerboard Power!

When a string is played with no fingers on the fingerboard, it is called an **open string**. Each open string has a letter name. Look at the open strings for each instrument in the string family.

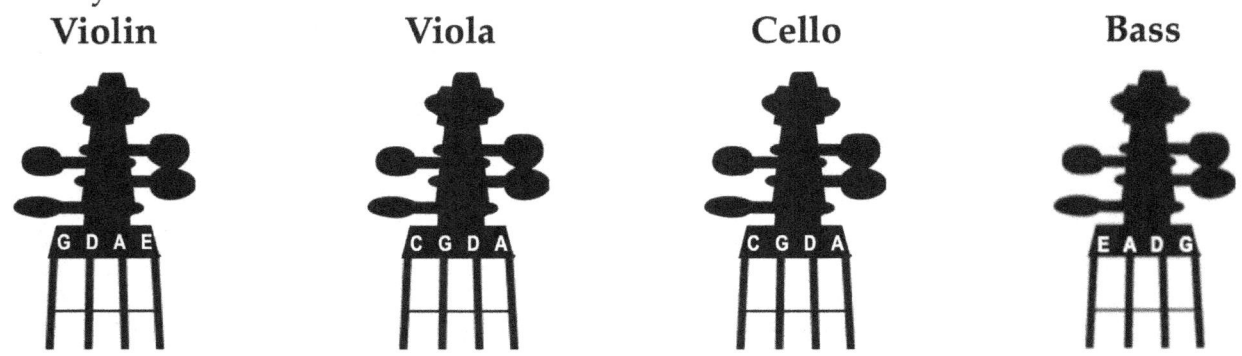

Violin	Viola	Cello	Bass
G D A E	C G D A	C G D A	E A D G

2. What instruments have the same open strings?

_____ and _____   _____ and _____

3. What is the difference between the violin and the double bass open strings?

_____

Each note on the fingerboard has a letter name. These are the letters on the D string and A string. Three of the letters have a # next to them. In music this is called a **sharp**. Say these letters C-sharp or F-sharp.

4. Write the letters in each house and the finger number in each circle.

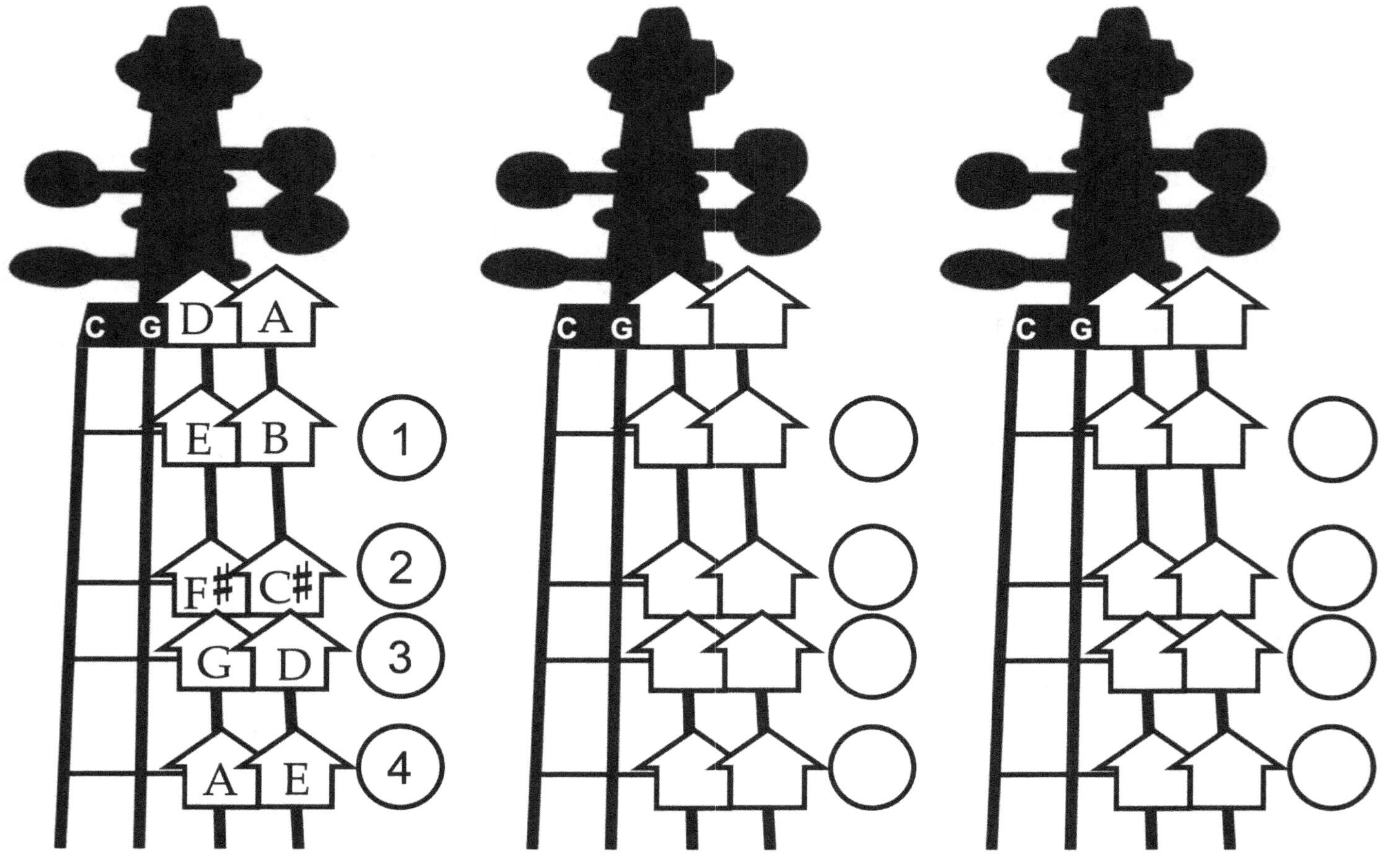

C G D A
E B ①
F# C# ②
G D ③
A E ④

C G

C G

The Magic of Music Theory Book 1 - © 2025 Horsehair Music. Photocopying prohibited.

What do you hear? #1

1. Color the string quartet while you listen to String Quartet No. 17 in B-flat, K. 458 "The Hunt" by Wolfgang Amadeus Mozart.

2. When you listen to this piece, does it sound like they are chasing something? In the space below draw a picture of a chase!

Lesson 3

Rhythm [rih-them] is how long or short we hold a pitch. Rhythm is measured and counted in beats. The number of beats each note gets is printed in the hearts.

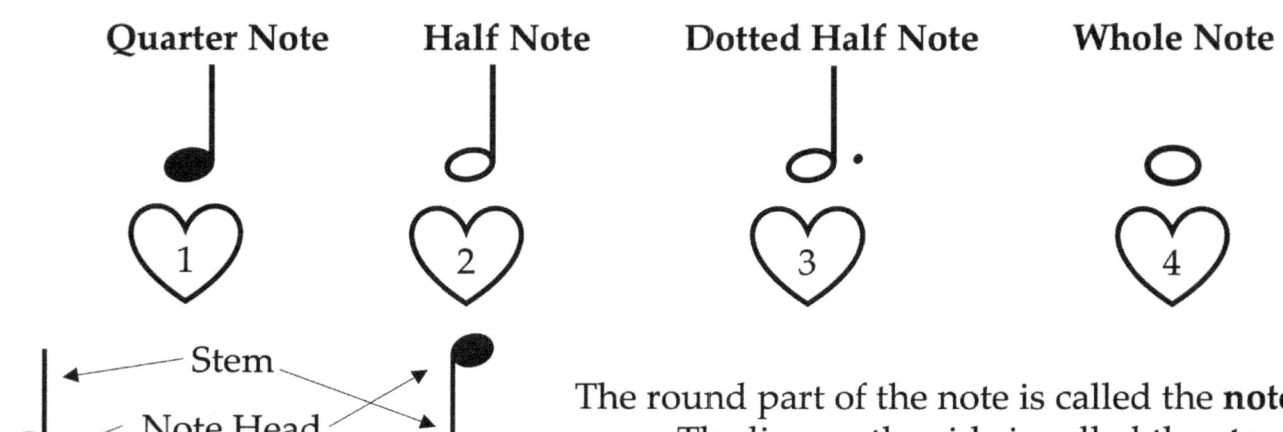

The round part of the note is called the **note head.** The line on the side is called the **stem.**

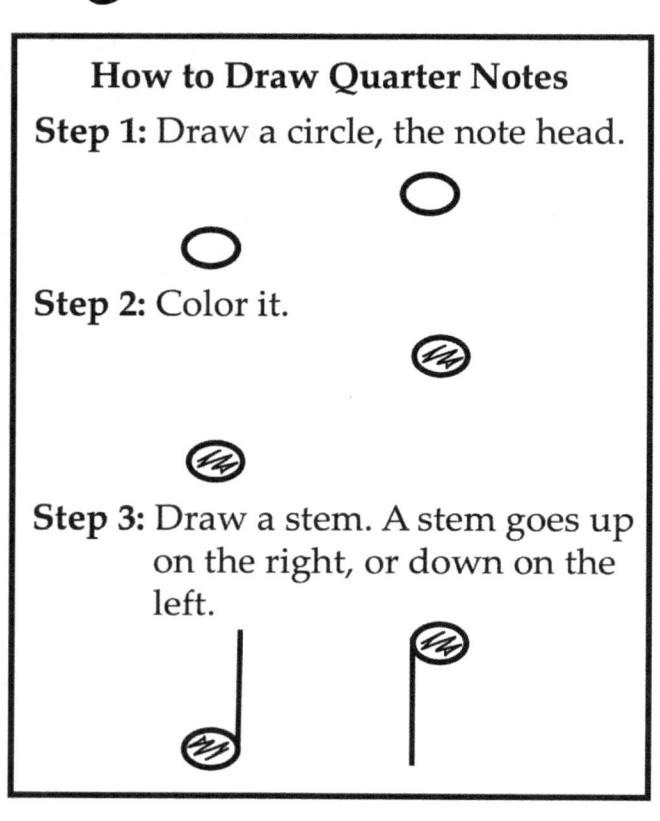

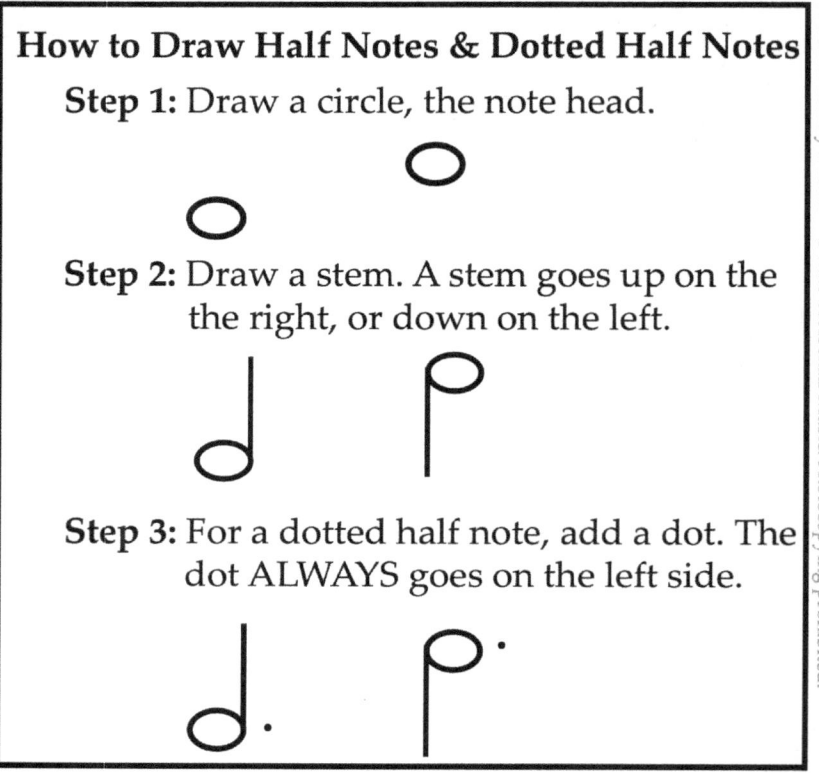

1. Draw the note in the box and write the number of beats each in the heart.

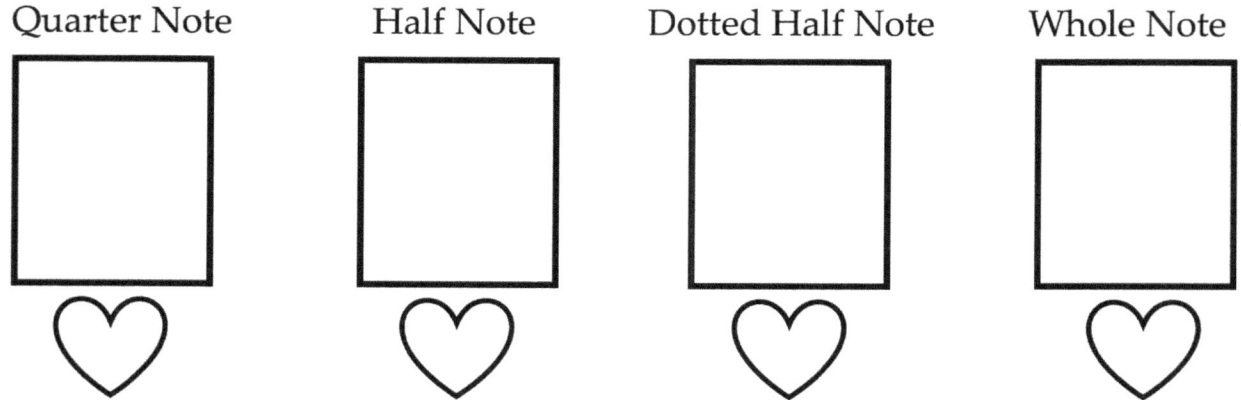

2. Draw the note in the box that equals the number of beats in each heart.

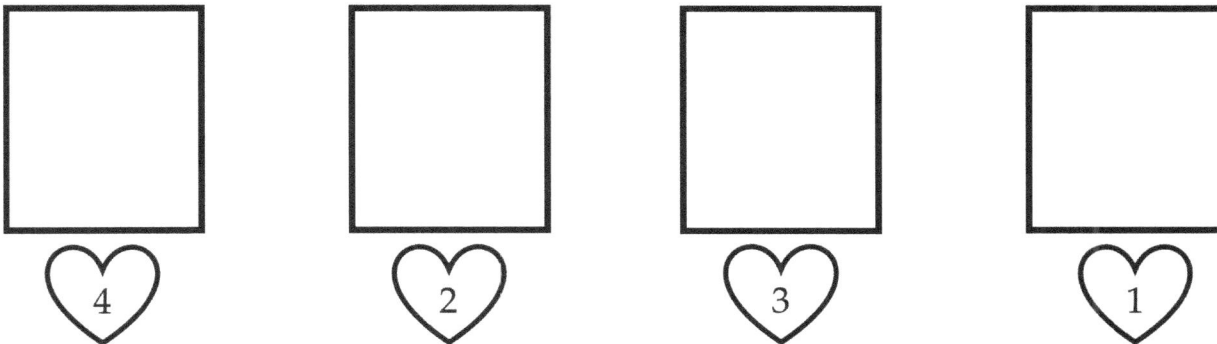

3. Add the number of beats in each equation and write the sum on the line. Then draw the note that equals that sum in the box.

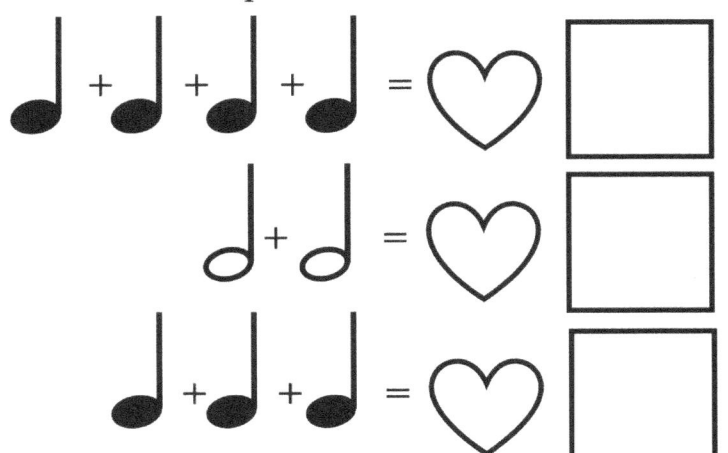

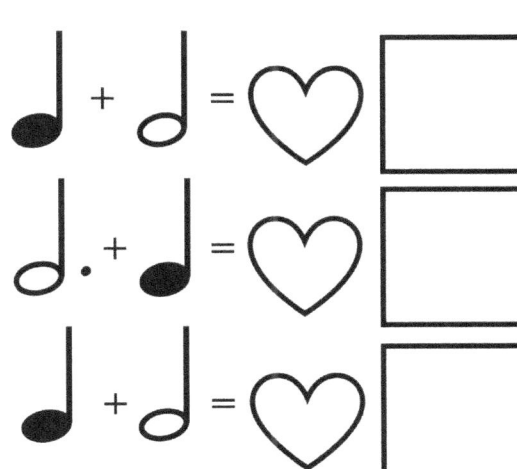

A **rest** tells us to stop playing. The bow stops moving on the string for a rest. A rest is just as important as the notes! Just like notes, each rest gets different number of beats.

Quarter Rest **Half Rest** **Whole Rest** 4. Draw a line from the rest to its matching note.

5. Draw the rests in each the box.

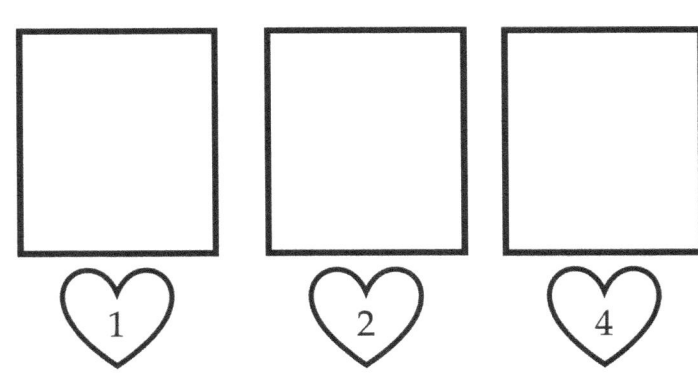

6. Which note does not have a matching rest?

_____

What do you hear? #2

You will hear several notes for each box. When you hear a long note, draw a line. When you hear a short note, draw a dot. Draw all the notes that you hear in the order that you hear them.

Long Note =   **Short Note =** ●

1.

2.

3.

4.

Choose from these examples.

The Magic of Music Theory Book 1 - © 2025 Horsehair Music. Photocopying prohibited.

Lesson 4

This is a **staff.** The staff has **5 lines and 4 spaces**. Always count the lines and spaces on the staff from **bottom to top!**

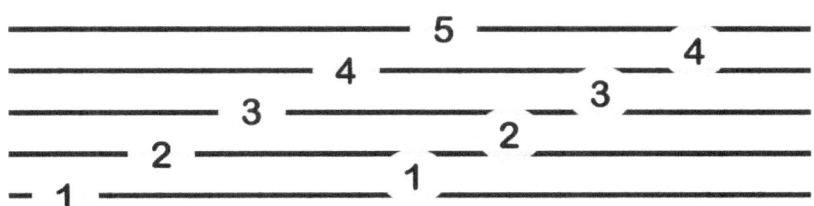

1. Write the numbers on the lines.

2. Write in the numbers in the spaces.

A **space note** sits between two lines. A **line note** has a line going through the middle of the note head.

Space Note

To draw a whole note as a space note, draw the circle between the two lines. Do not let the circle go above or below the lines.

Line Note

To draw a whole note as a line note, draw the circle so the line goes through the middle of the circle.

3. Draw 3 different space notes on the staff.

4. Draw 3 different line notes on the staff.

5. Color the line notes red and the space notes green.

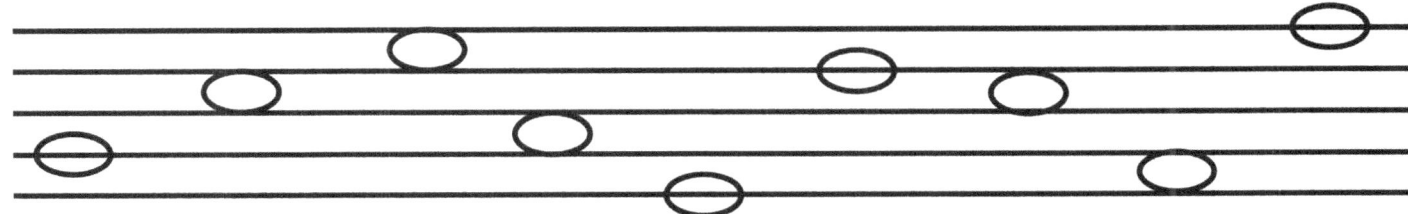

6. Write the line or space number for each note.

Line _____   Space _____

Line _____   Space _____

Line _____   Space _____   Line _____   Space _____

7. Draw a whole note on the correct line or space.

Line 3   Space 3   Line 4   Space 4

Space 2   Line 2   Space 1   Line 5

8. Always count the staff lines and spaces from _____ to _____.

16

The Magic of Music Theory Book 1 - © 2025 Horsehair Music. Photocopying prohibited.

Lesson 5

Dynamics means volume. We use Italian words to show what dynamic to play. **Forte** [for-tay] means loud. **Piano** [pee-an-o] means soft. **Mezzo Forte** [met-zo for-tay] means medium loud. **Mezzo Piano** [met-zo pee-an-o] means medium soft. Only the first letter of each word is written in italics in the music and is placed under the staff.

$\boldsymbol{f}$ = *forte* = loud $\boldsymbol{mf}$ = *mezzo forte* = medium loud

$\boldsymbol{p}$ = *piano* = soft $\boldsymbol{mp}$ = *mezzo piano* = medium soft

1. Circle *f, mf, mp,* or *p* to describe the dynamic in each picture.

f mf mp p	*f mf mp p*	*f mf mp p*
f mf mp p	*f mf mp p*	*f mf mp p*
f mf mp p	*f mf mp p*	*f mf mp p*

Crescendo [creh-shen-dough] means to play gradually louder. **Diminuendo** [dih-min-you-en-dough] means to play gradually softer. A crescendo or a diminuendo sign looks like an alligator mouth! The small, narrow end of the symbol is the soft side. The wide-open end of the symbol is the loud side.

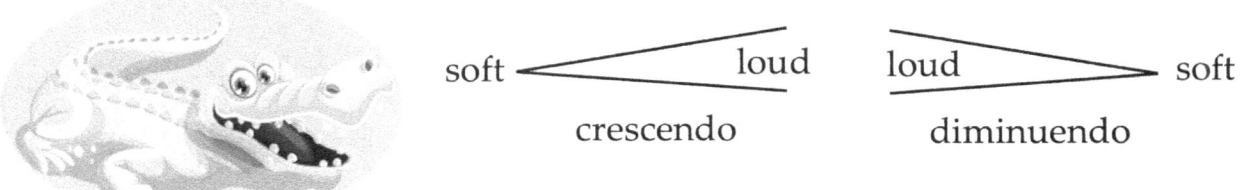

soft ————————— loud   loud ————————— soft
crescendo   diminuendo

What do you hear? #3

Circle the dynamic you hear.

1.	2.	3.
f *mf* *p*	*f* *mf* *p*	*f* *mf* *p*

Circle the correct dynamic if the notes you hear crescendo, or diminuendo.

4.	5.	6.
crescendo *diminuendo*	*crescendo* *diminuendo*	*crescendo* *diminuendo*

You will hear a pattern on an open string. Color the house of the string that you hear.

7.

8.

9.

* Additional ear training exercises can be found on p. 96 & 97

Choose one example for questions 1 – 3 and play with an exaggerated dynamic.

Johann Sebastian Bach – March

Ludwig van Beethoven – Symphony No. 5
I. Allegro con brio

Franz Joseph Haydn – "Surprise" Symphony
II. Andante

Choose one example for questions 4 – 6 and exaggerate the dynamic change.

Luigi Boccherini – Minuet

Wolfgang Amadeus Mozart – Requiem
Lacrimosa

Johann Sebastian Bach – Brandenburg Concerto No. 5
I. Allegro

Choose an open string and play a rhythm pattern on that open string for question 7-9.

The Magic of Music Theory Book 1 - © 2025 Horsehair Music. Photocopying prohibited.

Lesson 6

1. Use a colored pencil or crayon and trace the dotted line on line 3.

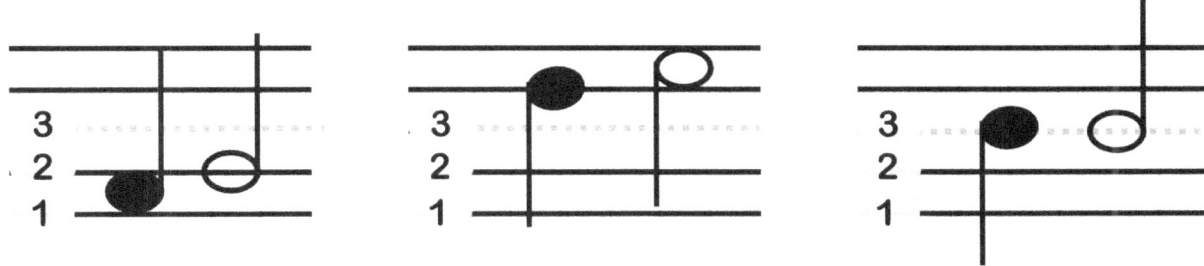

STEM RULES: If the note is **BELOW line 3, the stem goes UP on the right.**
If the note is **ABOVE line 3, the stem goes DOWN on the left.**
If the note is **on line 3, the stem can go up or down!**
Draw the stem through 3 lines or 3 spaces.

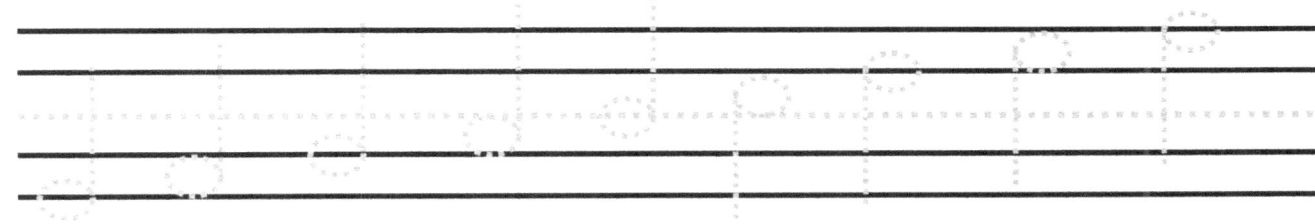

2. Use a red pencil or crayon and trace line 3 on the staff.
3. Trace the notes. Color in the note heads to make them quarter notes.

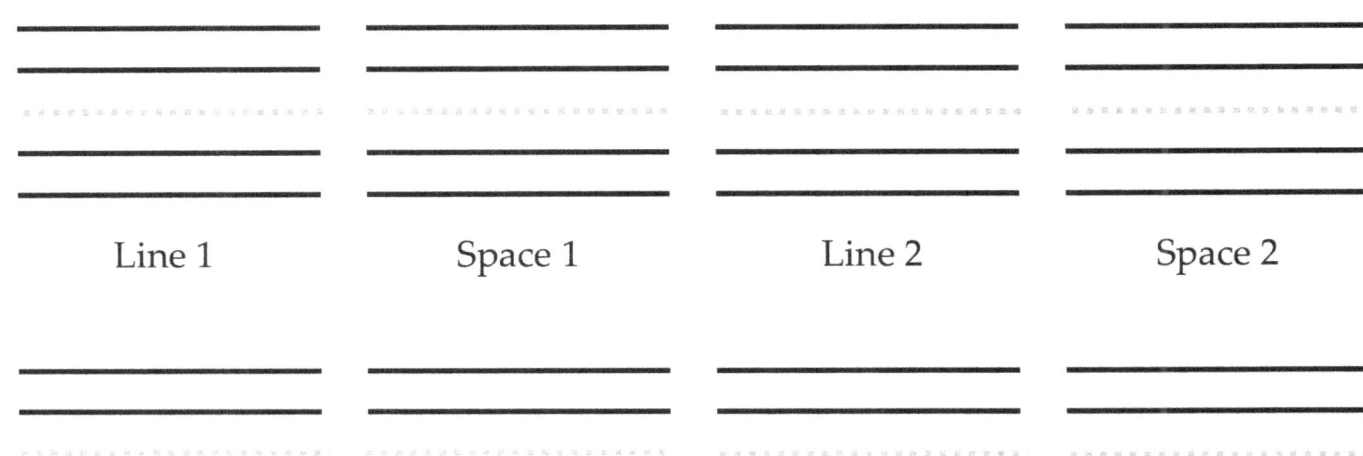

4. Trace line 3 with a red pencil. Then draw a quarter note on the correct line or space.

Line 1   Space 1   Line 2   Space 2

Line 3   Space 3   Line 4   Space 4   19

6. Draw a half note on the correct line or space.

Line 5   Space 4   Line 4   Space 3

Line 3   Space 2   Line 2   Space 1

7. A quarter rest is between line 2 and 4. Trace the quarter rests. Then draw 3 quarter rests.

8. A half rest sits on line 3. (It is in space 3 but does not touch line 4.) Trace the half rests. Then draw 3 half rests.

9. A whole rest hangs from line 4. (It is in space 3 but does not touch line 3.) Trace the whole rests. Then draw 3 whole rests.

10. If a note is above line 3, the stem goes _____ on the _____.

If a note is below line 3, the stem goes _____ on the _____.

Lesson 7

1. Draw a quarter note on the correct line or space with the correct stem direction

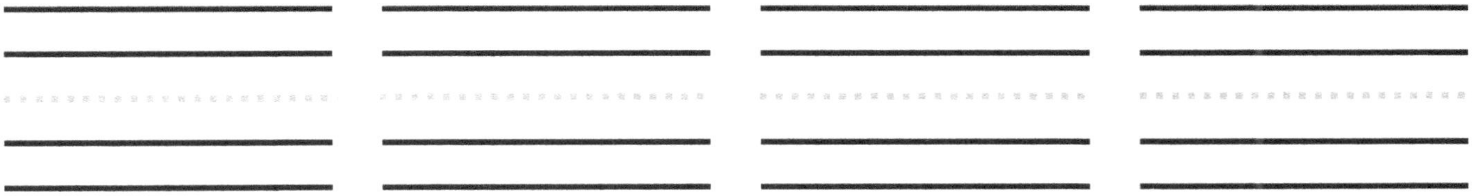

Line 4   Space 1   Line 2   Space 4

2. Write one letter of the music alphabet on each door beginning on G.

3. How many doors are there? _____ There are 8 letters from "G" to "G"!

Fingerboard Power! Each finger on the G string has a letter name. As we set fingers onto the fingerboard, we go forward through the music alphabet starting on G.

4. Write the letter in each house and finger number in the circle.

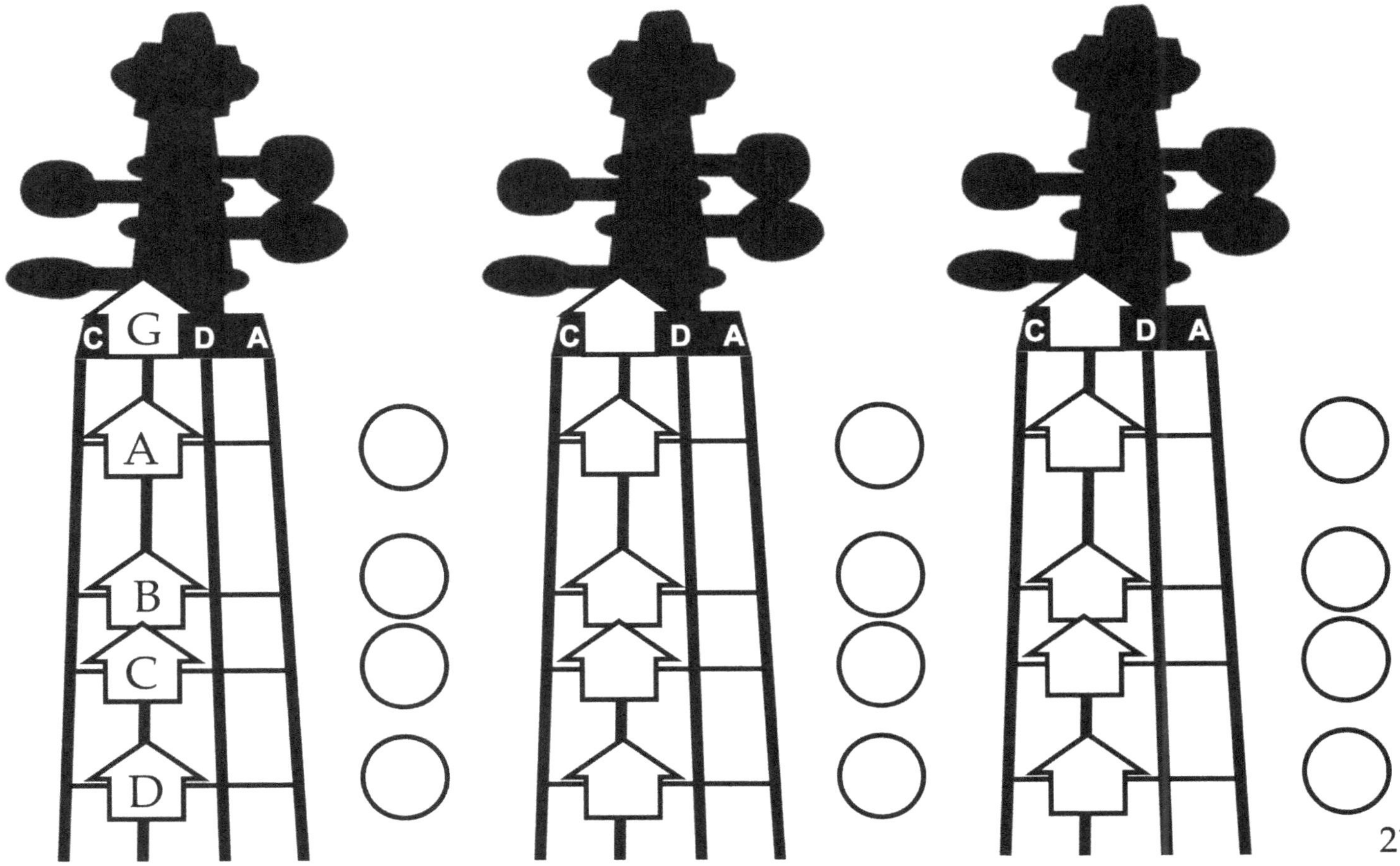

What do you hear? #4

You will hear 3 notes. If the notes go up, color the thumbs up. If the notes stay the same, color the sideways thumb. If the notes go down, color the thumbs down.

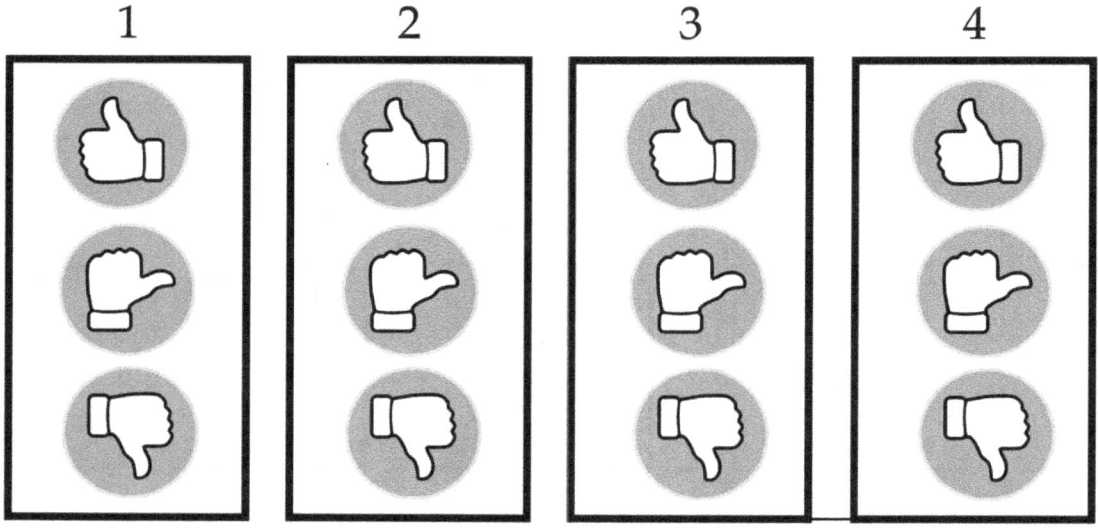

You will hear 2 melodies. If the melodies are the same, circle SAME. If the melodies are different, circle DIFFERENT.

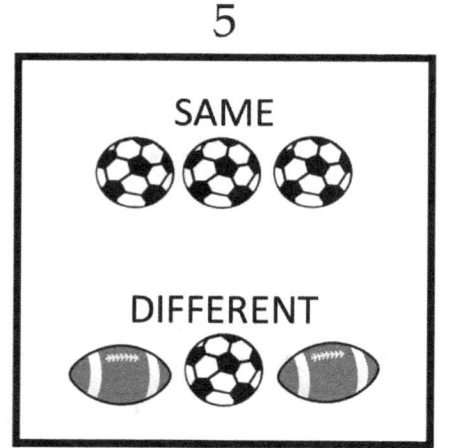
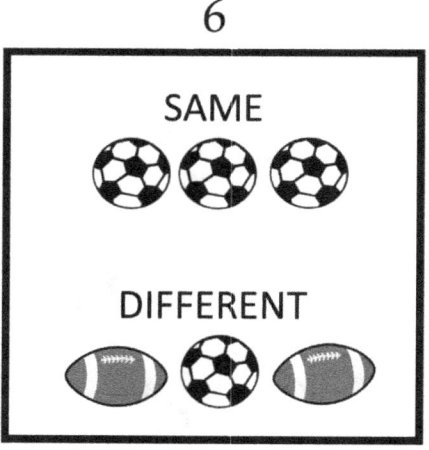
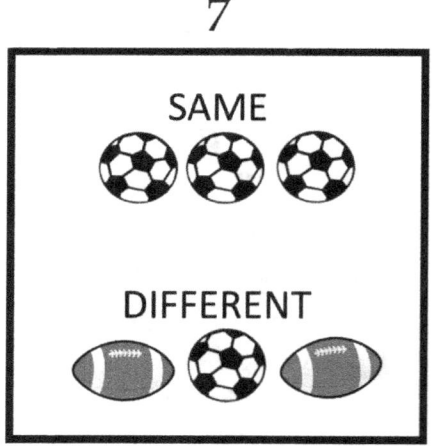

Additional ear training exercises can be found on p. 98.

Choose from these examples for questions 1-4.

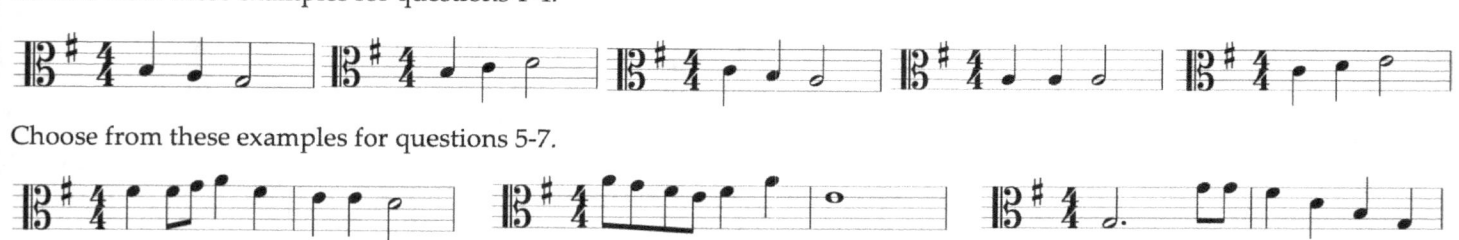

Choose from these examples for questions 5-7.

Lesson 8

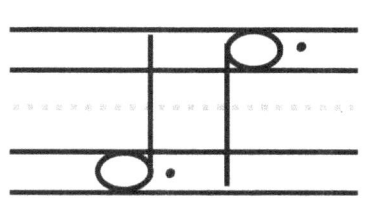 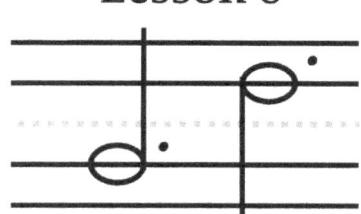 

DOT RULES: The dot is ALWAYS on the right side of the note head.
For a space note, the dot is in the same space as the note head.
For a line note, the dot goes in the space above the note head.

1. Draw a dotted half note on the correct line or space with the correct stem and dot.

Line 1   Space 1   Line 2   Space 2

Line 3   Space 3   Line 4   Space 4

Treble Clef

Violinists read music in the **treble clef**. **Treble** means high. The treble clef shows the high notes on the staff. It is also called the "G-Clef."

Alto Clef   Tenor Clef

The **alto clef** and the **tenor clef** are the same symbol! This clef is also called the "C-Clef." The little arrow in the middle points to where C lives. Violists read music in the alto clef.

Bass Clef

This is the **bass clef.** We pronounce the name, "bass," like "base" in baseball. Sometimes it is called the "F-Clef." Cellists and bassists read music in the bass clef.

2. Draw each step in the empty staff.

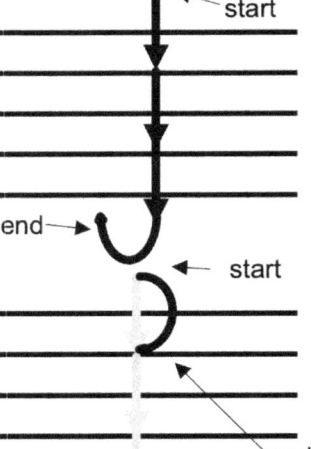

Step 1: First draw a **VERY TALL J.**

Step 2: Then draw a **Capital D** from the top of the J to touch line 4.

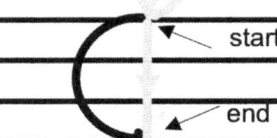

Step 3: Then draw a **BIG C**, from line 4 to touch the "tall J" at line 1.

Step 4: Draw another **BIG Capital D** from the bottom of line 1 to touch line 3.

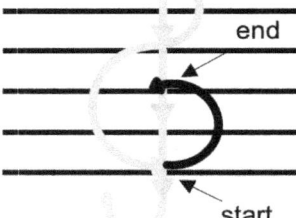

Step 5: Then add a **little C** around line 2.

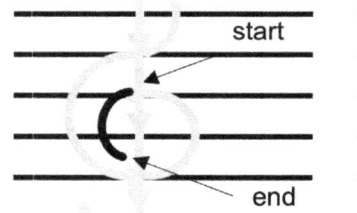

3. Draw a treble clef on each staff below.

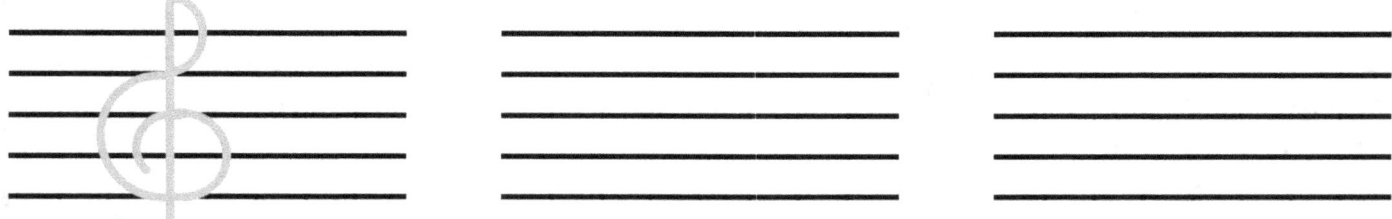

The Magic of Music Theory Book 1 - © 2025 Horsehair Music. Photocopying prohibited.

Lesson 9

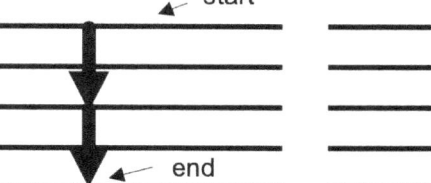

How to Draw an Alto Clef or "C-Clef"

1. Draw each step in the empty staff.
   Step 1: Draw a thick line from line 5 to line 1.

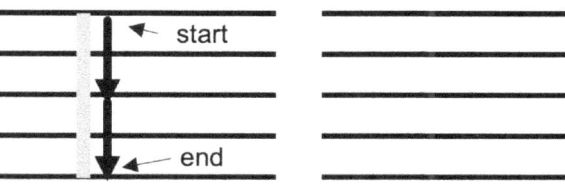

   Step 2: Draw a thin line on the right side of the thick line.

   Step 3: Draw a **Backwards C**, starting on line 5, ending in space 3. Leave a little space between the line and the **C**.

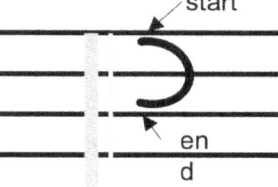

   Step 4: Draw a **Sideways V** with the point of the **V** on line 3.

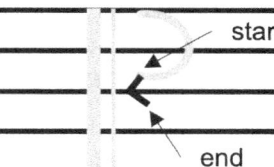

   Step 5: Draw a **Backwards C** starting at the end of the **V** in space 2.

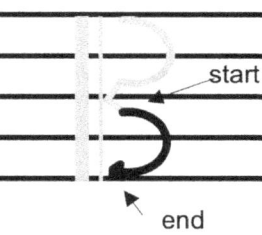

2. Trace the alto clef on each staff.

3. Draw an alto clef on each staff.

4. Draw each step in the empty staff.

Step 1: Draw a **Big Dot** on line 4.

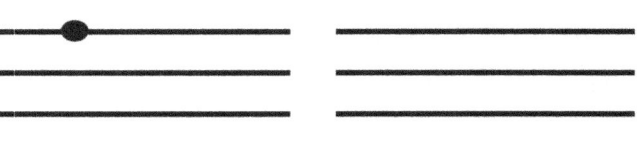

Step 2: Draw **Half of a Heart** starting on the dot ending in space 1, but not touching line 1.

Step 3: Draw a **Dot** on the right side in space 4.

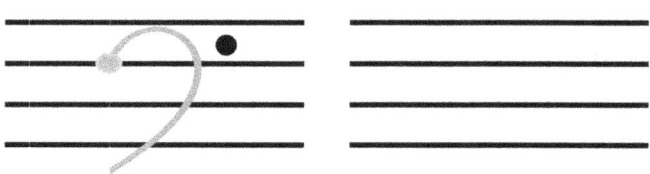

Step 3: Draw a **Dot** on the right side in space 3.

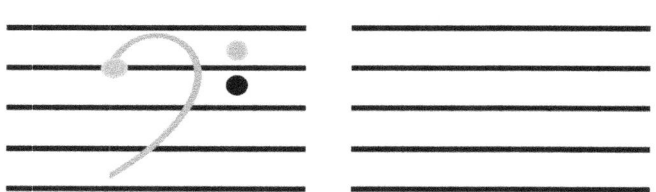

5. Trace a bass clef on each staff below.

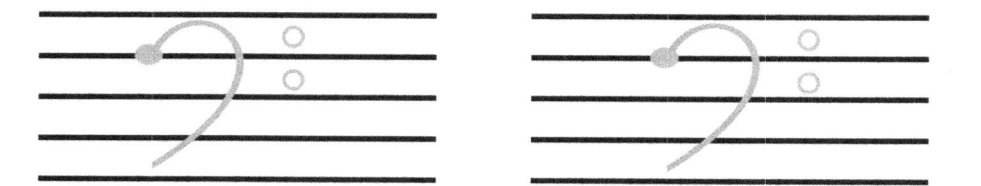

6. Draw a bass clef on each staff.

Lesson 10

1. Write one letter of the music alphabet in each house starting with A.

Each letter of the music alphabet also has a staff house.

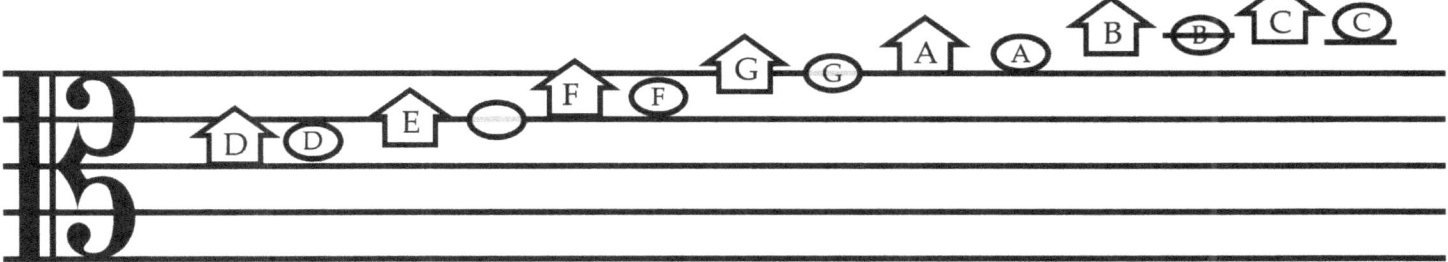

Notice that the notes and letters both step up as they get higher on the staff. The music alphabet letters move from a line to the very next space. Then, from the space to the very next line.

2. Write in the line or space number in each bubble from bottom to top. Then, circle if the note is on a line or space. Finally, write the line or space number in the blank. The first one is done for you.

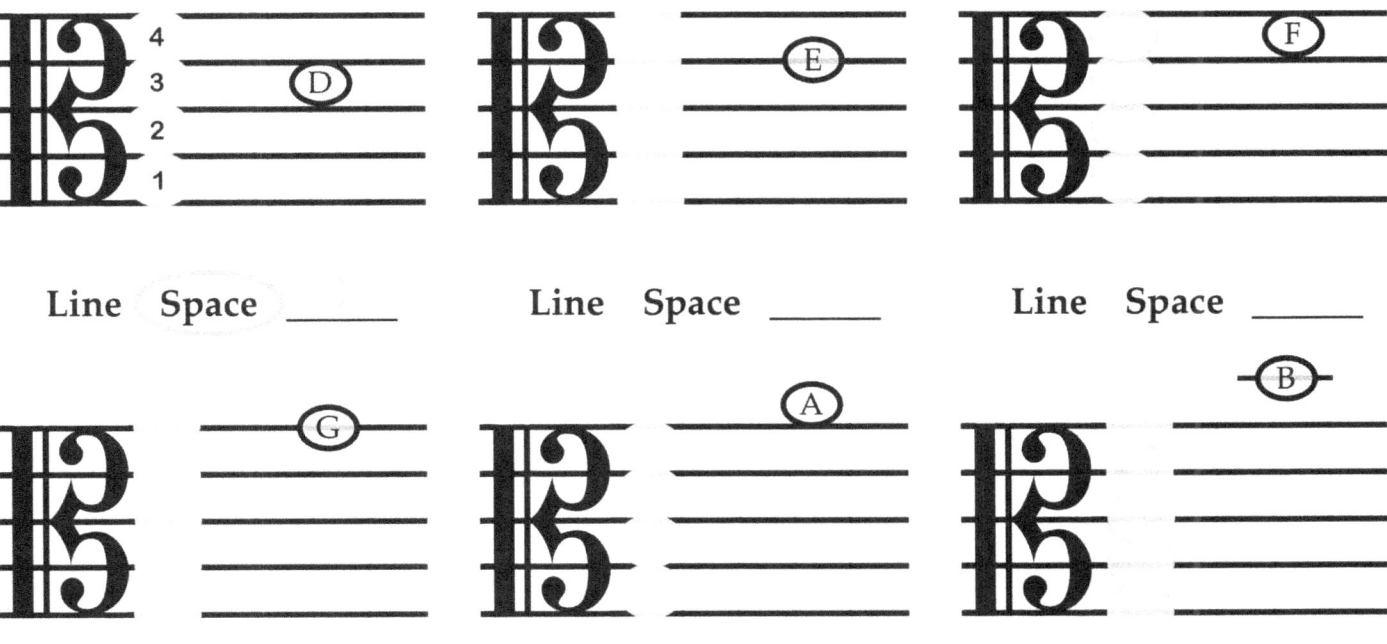

3. It's a neighborhood house painting party! Follow the color guide and make each house on the fingerboard the correct color!

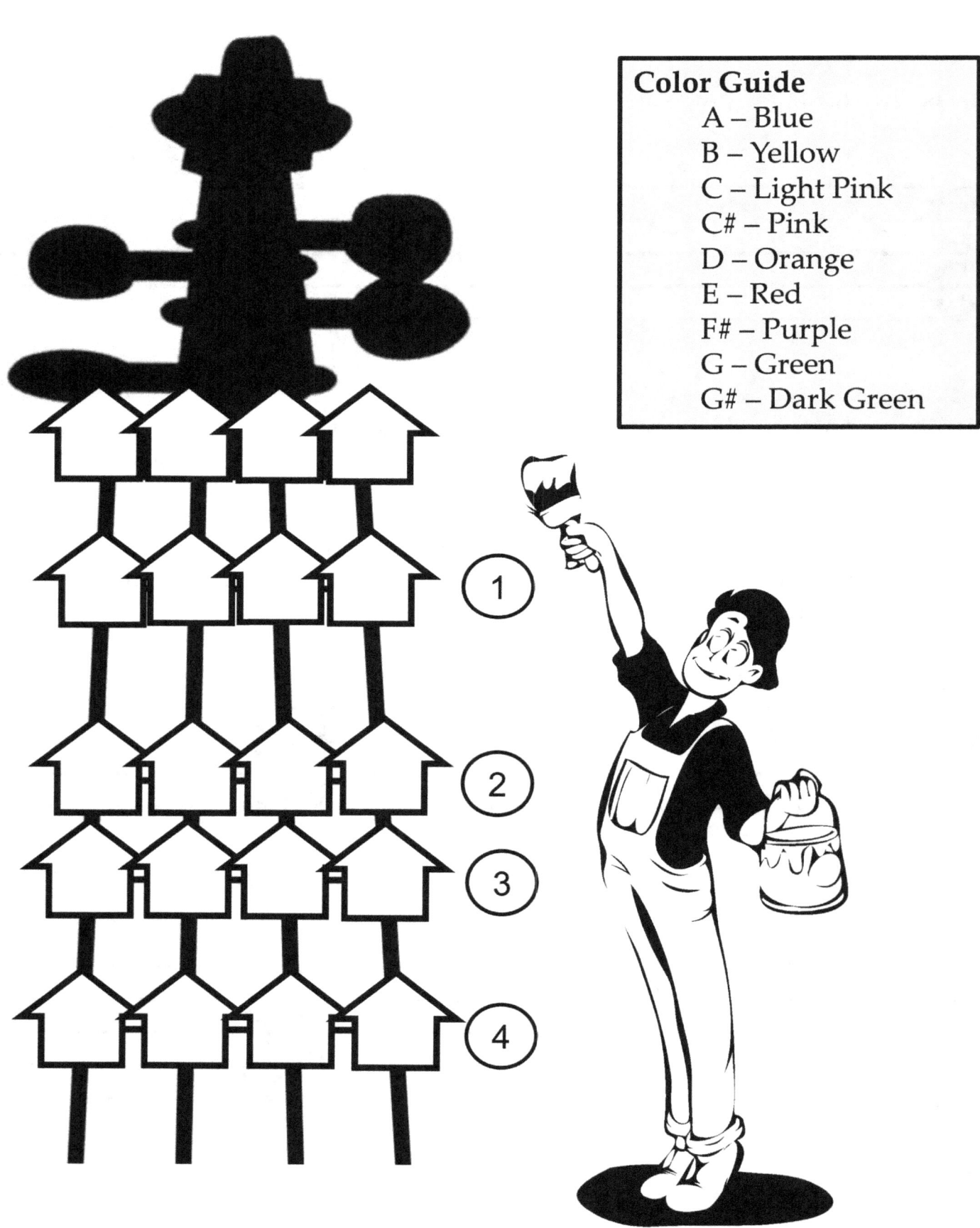

Color Guide
A – Blue
B – Yellow
C – Light Pink
C# – Pink
D – Orange
E – Red
F# – Purple
G – Green
G# – Dark Green

Lesson 11

Each house on the fingerboard has a matching "house" (place) on the staff.

1. Draw a line from the fingerboard house to its staff house.

The staff can be extended higher or lower by adding little lines called **ledger lines.**

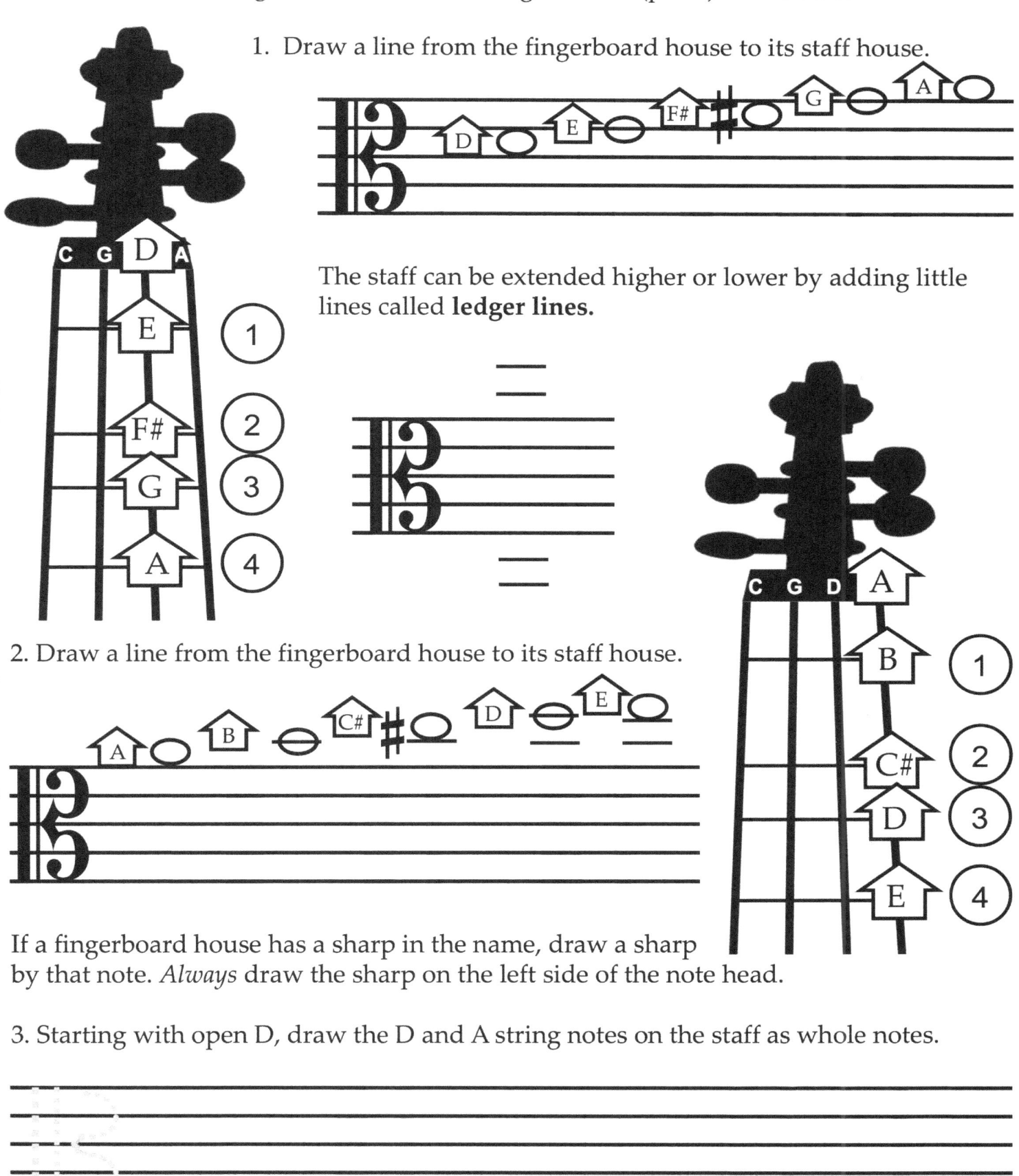

2. Draw a line from the fingerboard house to its staff house.

If a fingerboard house has a sharp in the name, draw a sharp by that note. *Always* draw the sharp on the left side of the note head.

3. Starting with open D, draw the D and A string notes on the staff as whole notes.

Discover the Composers

Fill in the letter name to learn about the life of a great composer while you listen to String Quartet No. 2 by Florence Price.

___lor___n___e ___e___trice Pri___e was ___orn in Arkansas

in 1887. She is the ___irst ___frican-___meri___an woman to ___e

reco___nized as an or___h___stra ___omposer. Her music w___s

___lmost lost ___n___ ___or___otten. In 2009 ___ozens of her

pieces w___re ___is___overed ___t her summ___r home

n___ ___r Chi___ ___ ___o. She wrot___ over 400 ___ompositions.

Lesson 12

1. Follow the steps to draw each D and A string note.
   - ❑ Trace line 3.
   - ❑ Trace the alto clef.
   - ❑ Trace the first quarter note. Then draw 4 more quarter notes on the staff.
   - ❑ Write the finger number in each blank.

Letter Name: D D D D D

Finger Number: ___ ___ ___ ___ ___

Letter Name: E E E E E

Finger Number: ___ ___ ___ ___ ___

The sharp on the left

Letter Name: F# F# F# F# F#

Finger Number: ___ ___ ___ ___ ___

Letter Name: G G G G G

Finger Number: ___ ___ ___ ___ ___

Letter Name: A   A   A   A   A
Finger Number: ____   ____   ____   ____   ____

Letter Name: B   B   B   B   B
Finger Number: ____   ____   ____   ____   ____

Letter Name: C#   C#   C#   C#   C#
Finger Number: ____   ____   ____   ____   ____

Letter Name: D   D   D   D   D
Finger Number: ____   ____   ____   ____   ____

Letter Name: E   E   E   E   E
32 Finger Number: ____   ____   ____   ____   ____

Save the Vegetables!

These vegetables will get chopped up and eaten for dinner unless you help them get through the maze to the refrigerator! They may only pass through A string notes. If they pass through a D string note, Chef Sautillé [so-tee-aye] will chop them up!

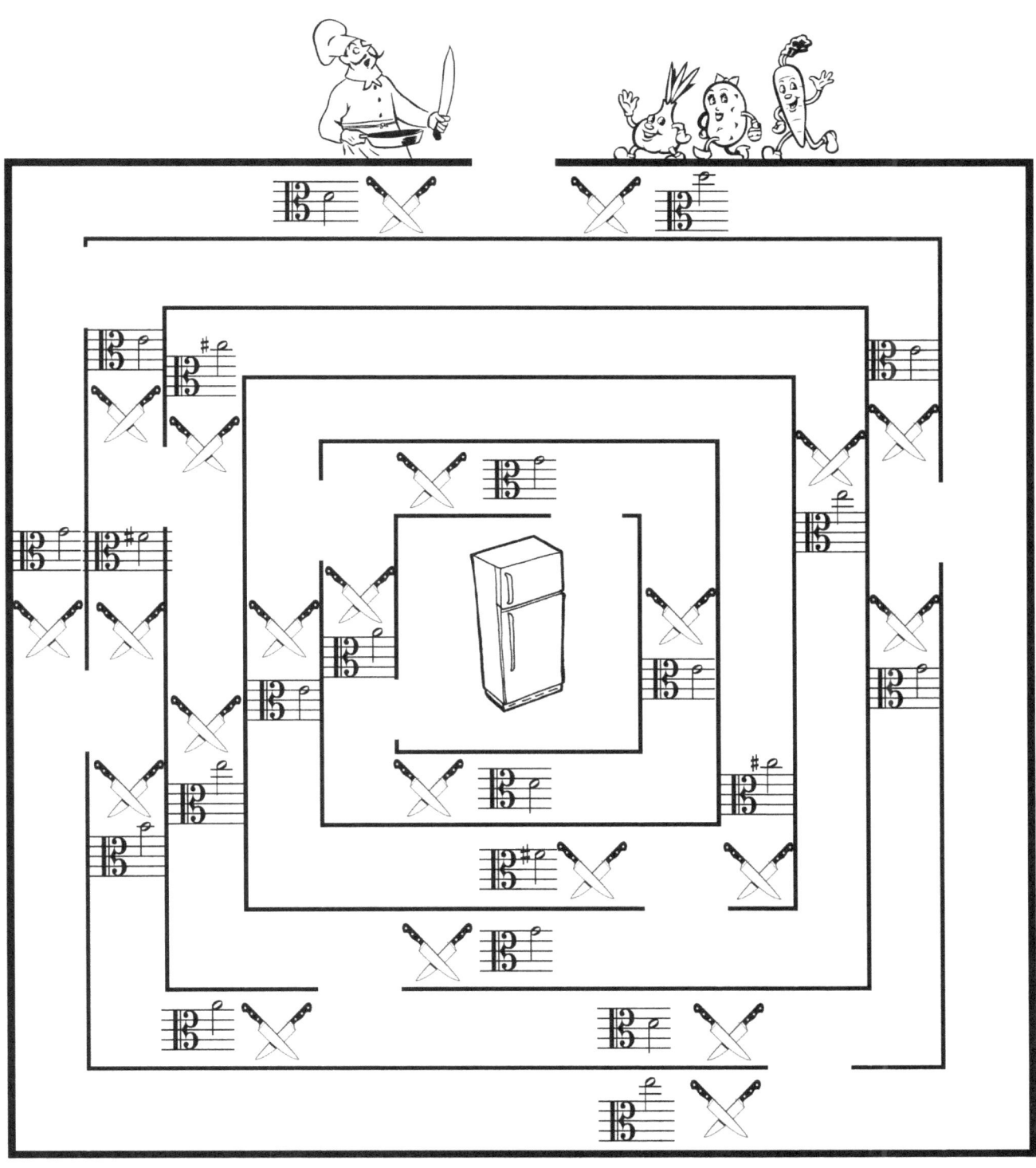

Lesson 13

The G string fingerboard houses have matching staff houses.

Open G is a space note in space 1.

1. Trace the alto clef.
   Draw 3 G whole notes on the staff.
   Write the letter below

_____ _____ _____

G (space 1) – step up – land on **A** (line 2).

2. Trace the alto clef.
   Draw 3 A whole notes on the staff.
   Write the letter below.

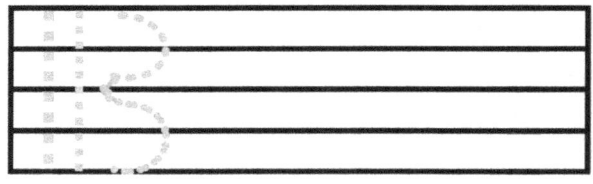

_____ _____ _____

A (line 2) – step up – land on **B** (space 2).

3. Trace the alto clef.
   Draw 3 B whole notes on the staff.
   Write the letter below.

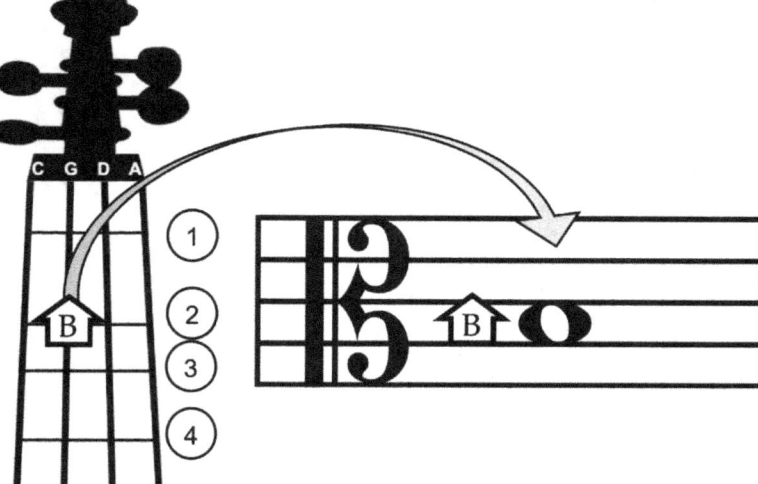

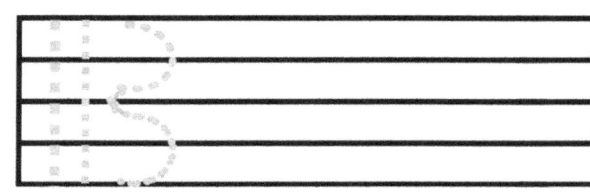

_____ _____ _____

B (space 2) – step up – land on **C** (line 3).

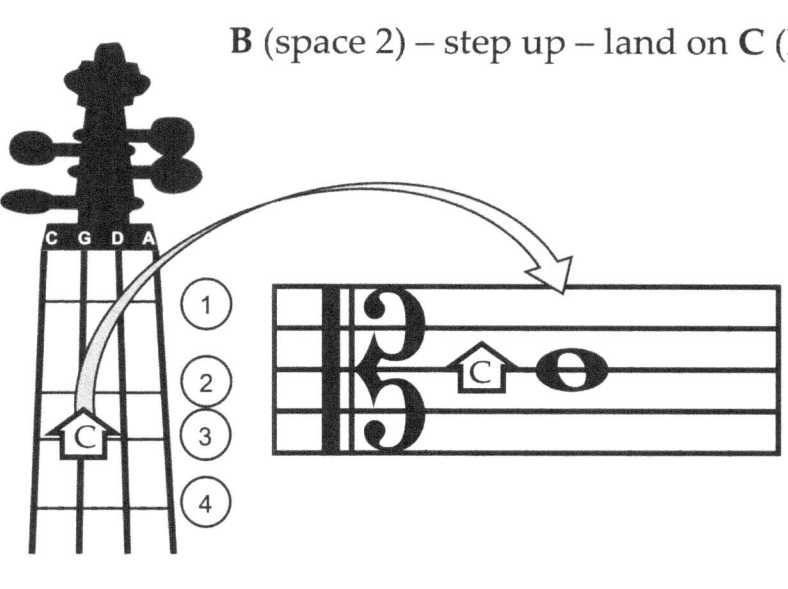

4. Trace the alto clef.
   Draw 3 C whole notes on the staff.
   Write the letter below.

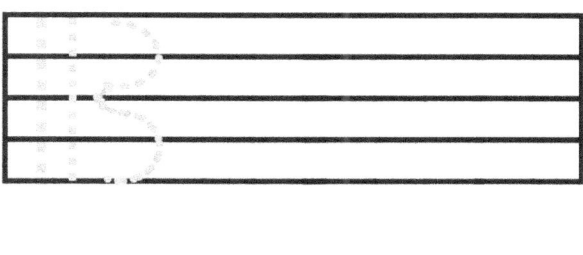

____ ____ ____

C (line 3) – step up – land on **D** (space 3).

5. Trace the alto clef.
   Draw 3 D whole notes on the staff.
   Write the letter below.

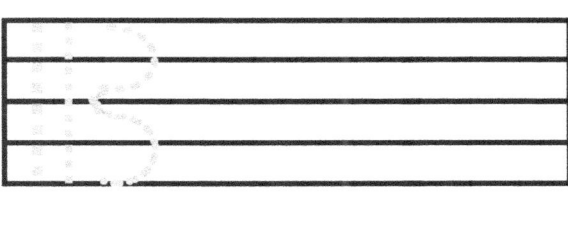

____ ____ ____

6. Draw an alto clef at the beginning of the staff.

7. Draw each G string note as a whole note in each measure.

8. Write the finger number for each note on the line.

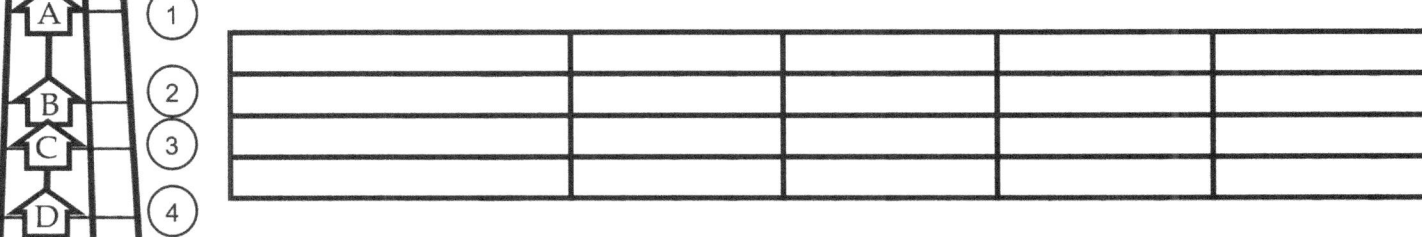

Letter Name: __G__ __A__ __B__ __C__ __D__

Finger Number: ____ ____ ____ ____ ____

Discover the Composers

Fill in the letter name to learn about the life of a great composer while you listen to String Quartet in A Major, Op. 15, No. 6 by Francois Gossec.

Fr___n___ois ___osse___ w___s from ___el___ium. He

le___rne___ to play violin and h___rpsi___hor___. At a___e 17

he went to Fr___n___e to study music and be___an playing violin

in the or___hestr___. Then ___ ___reed to ___e the ___on___uctor!

___osse___ wrote 30 symphonies, some oper___s, an___ ___

lar___e ___mount of ___h___m___er musi___.

Lesson 14

1. Follow the steps to draw each G string note.
   - ❑ Trace line 3.
   - ❑ Trace the alto clef.
   - ❑ Trace the first dotted half note. Then draw 4 more dotted half notes.
   - ❑ Write the finger number in each blank.

Letter Name: __G__   __G__   __G__   __G__   __G__

Finger Number: ____   ____   ____   ____   ____

Letter Name: __A__   __A__   __A__   __A__   __A__

Finger Number: ____   ____   ____   ____   ____

Letter Name: __B__   __B__   __B__   __B__   __B__

Finger Number: ____   ____   ____   ____   ____

Letter Name: __C__   __C__   __C__   __C__   __C__

Finger Number: ____   ____   ____   ____   ____

Letter Name: __D__ __D__ __D__ __D__ __D__

Finger Number: ____ ____ ____ ____ ____

2. Draw the G string, D string, and A string notes as dotted half notes on the staff.

Letter Name: __G__ __A__ __B__ __C__ __D__ __E__ __F#__ __G__ __A__ __B__ __C#__ __D__ __E__

Finger Number: __ __ __ __ __or__ __ __ __ __or__ __ __ __ __

3. Draw the symbol for each term in the box.

Crescendo [ ]

Forte [ ]

Piano [ ]

Diminuendo [ ]

Mezzo Piano [ ]

Mezzo Forte [ ]

?? **Did you know?** Sound is created by waves in the air. These are called **sound waves**. The closer the sound waves are to each other, the higher the pitch will be. If the sound waves are farther apart, the pitch moves lower. The number of sound waves occurring in one second of time is called the **frequency**. When a thick string is plucked or bowed, it vibrates more slowly and the sound waves are farther apart. This makes a low sound and has a low frequency. When a thin string is plucked or bowed, it vibrates faster and the sounds waves are closer together. This makes a high sound and has a high frequency. Frequency is measured in *hertz*. The viola's **open A string** is **440 hertz.** This means that there are 440 sound waves in 1 second!

Lesson 15

The C string fingerboard houses have matching houses on the staff.

Open C is a space note and is a space note under ledger line 1.

1. Trace the alto clef.
   Draw 1 ledger line and 3 C whole notes under the staff.
   Write the letter below.

_____   _____   _____

C (space under ledger line 1) – step up – land on **D** (ledger line 1).

2. Trace the alto clef.
   Draw 1 ledger line down and 3 D whole notes under the staff.
   Write the letter below.

_____   _____   _____

D (ledger line 1) – step up – land on **E** (space under the staff).

3. Trace the alto clef.
   Draw 3 E whole notes on the staff.
   Write the letter below.

_____   _____   _____

E (space under the staff) – step up – land on **F** (line 1).

4. Trace the alto clef.
   Draw 3 F whole notes on the staff.
   Write the letters below.

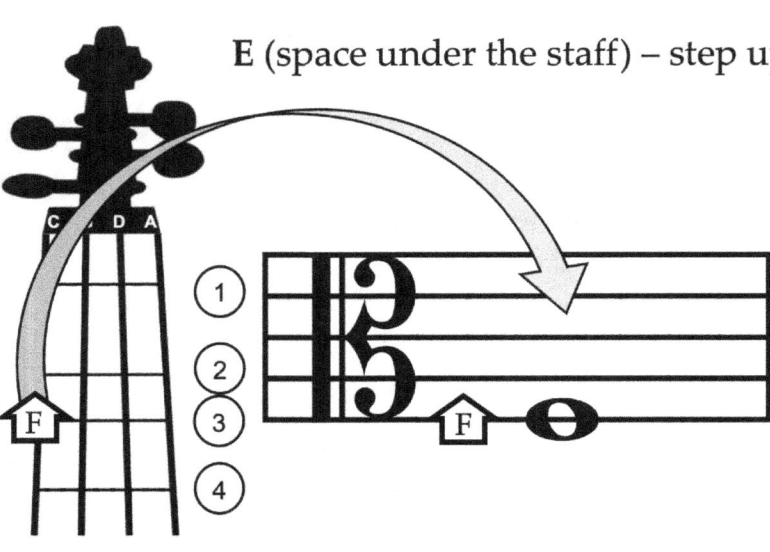

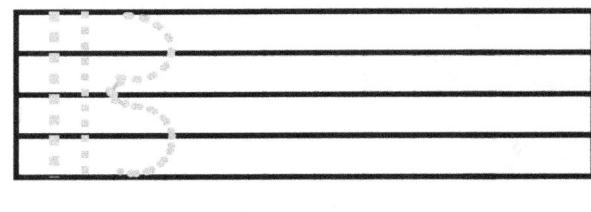

_____   _____   _____

F (line 1) – step up – land on **G** (space 1).

5. Trace the alto clef.
   Draw 3 G whole notes on the staff.
   Write the letters below.

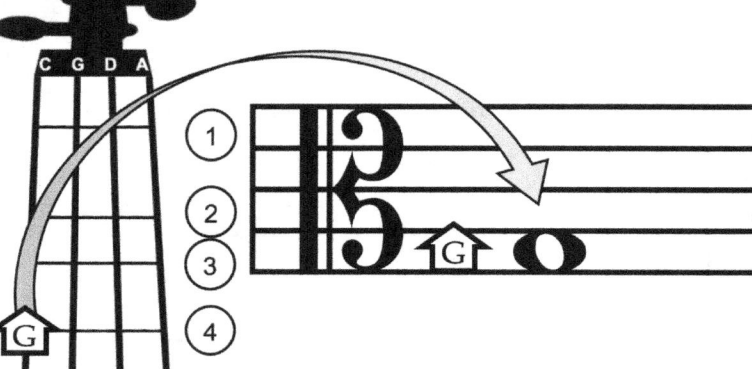

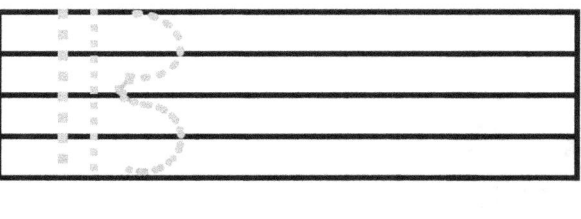

_____   _____   _____

6. Trace the alto clef at the beginning of the staff.

7. Draw each C string note as a whole note in each measure.

8. Write the finger number on the line under each note.

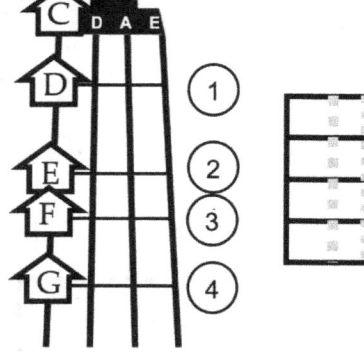

Letter Name: __C__   __D__   __E__   __F__   __G__

Finger Number: _____   _____   _____   _____   _____

The Magic of Music Theory Book 1 - © 2025 Horsehair Music. Photocopying prohibited.

Discover the Composers

Fill in the letter name to learn about the life of a great composer while you listen to String Quartet in E-flat Major, Op. 33, No. 2 by Franz Joseph Haydn.

Austrian ___omposr, ___ranz Joseph Hay___n be___an studying music

at 5 years old. He san___ in the boys ___hoir at ___hur___h. H___ learne___

to play harpsi___hor___ and or___an. He b ___ ___an ___omposing and

wrote over 200 pieces. He is call___d the "___ather o___ the strin___ quartet"

b___ ___ause he wrote so many. He also love___ a ___oo___ jok___.

Why did Mozart get rid of all his chickens?

They kept saying, Bach, Bach, Bach

Lesson 16

1. The little lines that extend the staff up or down are called _____ _____.

(p. 29)

2. The C string notes have stems going _____on the _____ side of the note head.

3. Follow the steps to draw each C string note.
   - ❏ Trace line 3.
   - ❏ Trace the alto clef.
   - ❏ Trace the first half note. Then draw 4 more half notes.
   - ❏ Write the finger number in each blank.

Letter Name: C   C   C   C   C

Finger Number: ____ ____ ____ ____ ____

Letter Name: D   D   D   D   D

Finger Number: ____ ____ ____ ____ ____

Letter Name: E   E   E   E   E

Finger Number: ____ ____ ____ ____ ____

Letter Name: F   F   F   F   F

Finger Number: ____ ____ ____ ____ ____

Letter Name: G   G   G   G   G

Finger Number: ____ ____ ____ ____ ____

4. You be the teacher! There are 3 errors in each line. Use a red crayon or colored pencil and circle each error that you find.

5. Color the C string barn yellow. Then color all the sheep with C string notes yellow.
6. Color the G string barn green. Then color all the sheep with G string notes green.
7. Color the D string barn red. Then color all the sheep with D string notes red.
8. Color the A string barn blue. Then color all the sheep with A string notes blue.

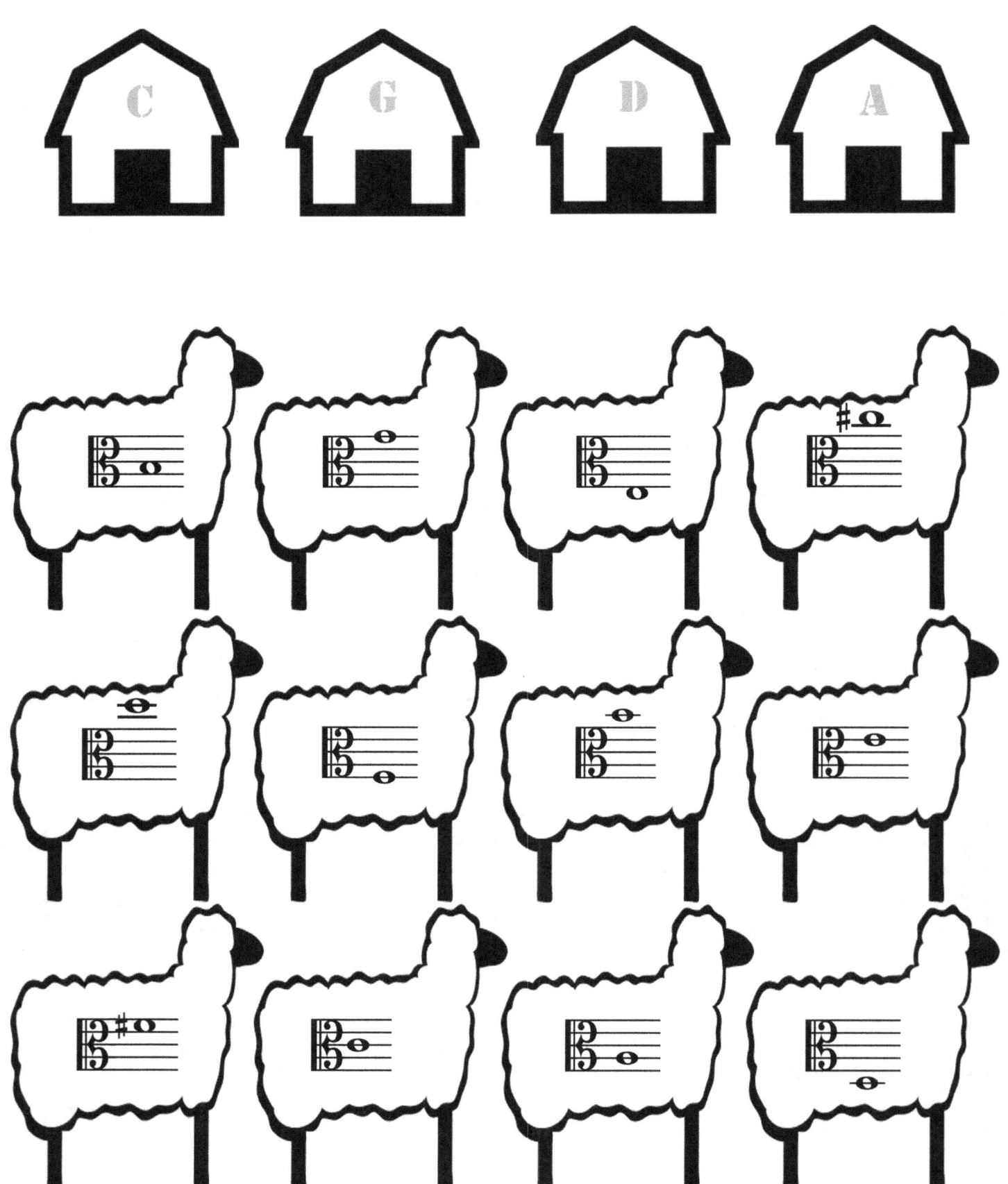

Music Note Bowling

Preparing to play:
1. Cut out each card and cut down the center on the dotted line.
2. Group the cards with staff notes in one pile, and the cards with bowling balls in another pile.
3. Take the staff note cards and spread them out on the floor or table face down.
4. Take the bowling ball cards and spread them out on the floor face down.

How to play with one player:
1. Turn one card over in each group. If the letter on the bowling ball does not match the staff note, turn both cards back over, face down.
2. Continue turning one card over in each group until you find a match.
3. Your goal is to match all the staff cards to the correct letter on the bowling ball card.

How to play with two or more players:
1. The first player turns over one bowling ball card and one staff card. If the cards match, that player takes both the cards and sets them aside. If the cards do not match, the player turns both cards over, and his turn is over.
2. If the player has a match, he takes another turn. If the player does not have a match, the next player takes a turn looking to find a match.
3. Continue until all the cards in both piles have been matched.

A and D string bowling cards can be found in Primer level.

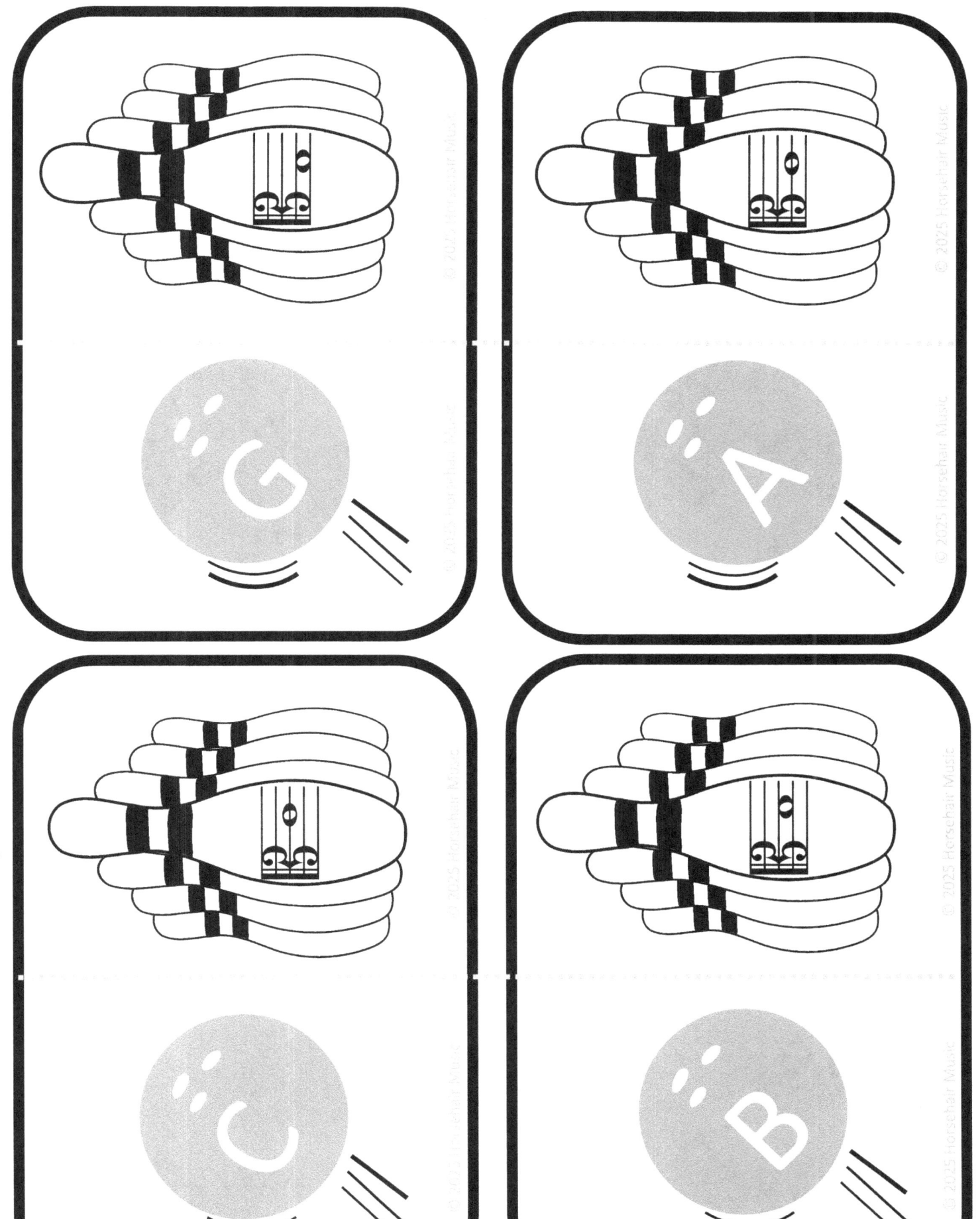

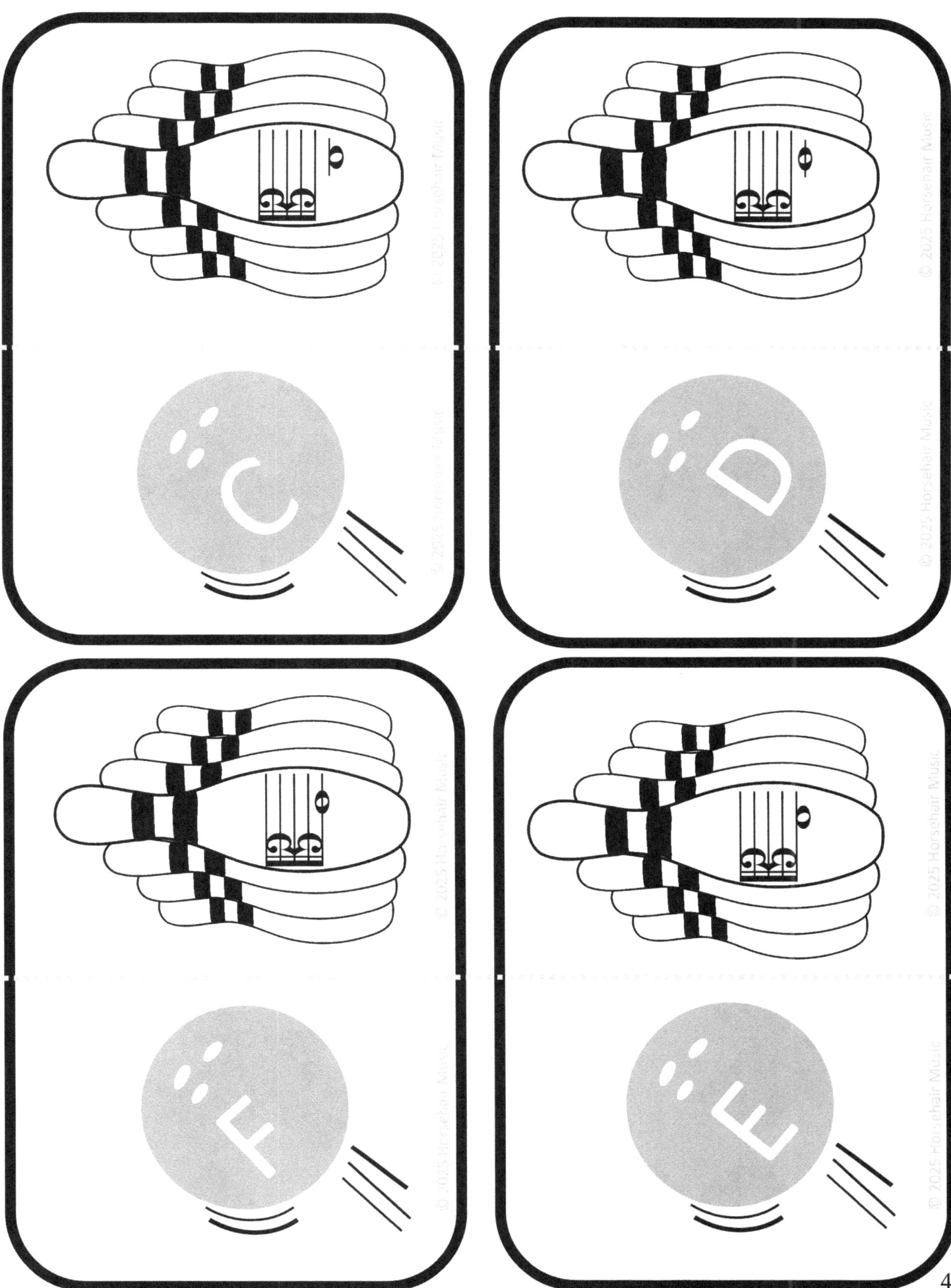

Lesson 17

To step up in the music alphabet, we move forward to the next letter. To step down in the music alphabet, we move backwards by one letter.

1. Fill in the blanks.

A – step up – land on _____   C – step up – land on _____   G – step down – land on _____

D – step up – land on _____   B – step down – land on _____   C – step up – land on _____

C – step down – land on _____   F – step up – land on _____   E – step up – land on _____

B – step up – land on _____   E – step down – land on _____   D – step up – land on _____

To step up we set fingers onto the fingerboard. To step down we lift fingers off the fingerboard.

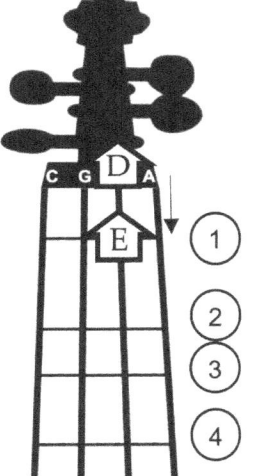

Step Up
To **step up** on the fingerboard, place the next finger onto the fingerboard.

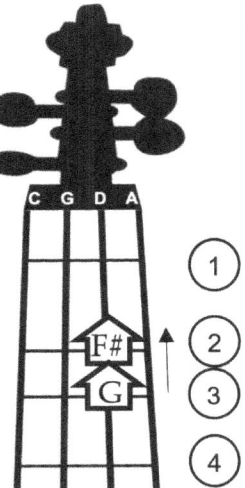

Step Down
To **step down** on the fingerboard, lift a finger off the fingerboard.

2. Draw two circles on each fingerboard that *step up* and *step down* from the printed house Then, write the letters in each circle. The first one is done for you.

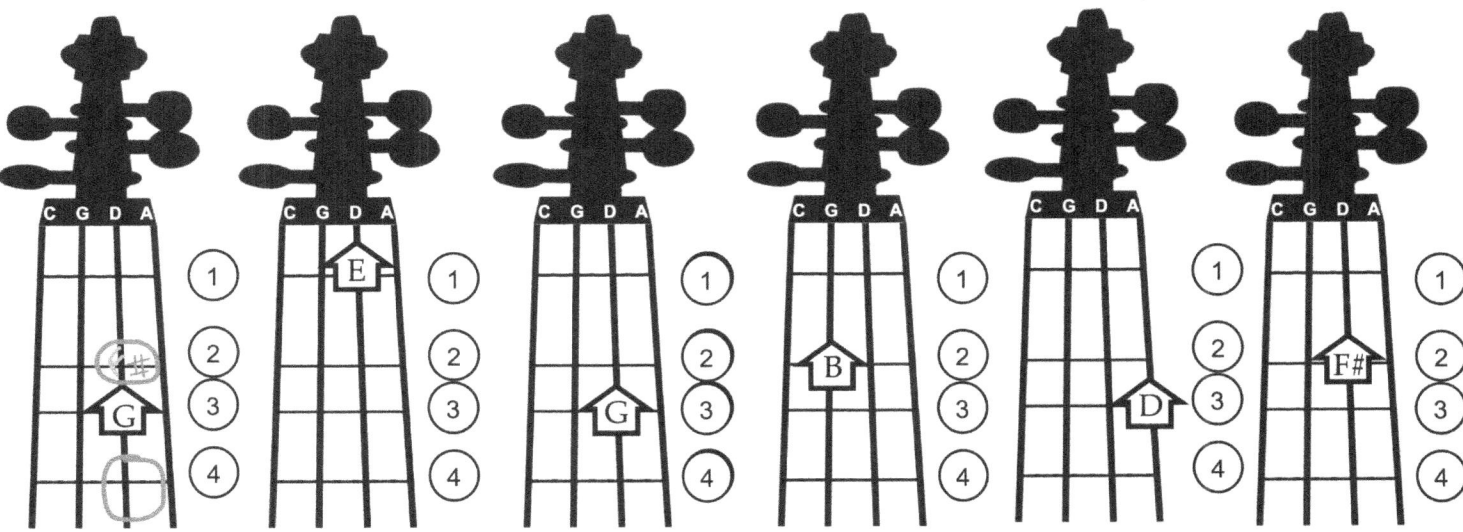

51

Wait a minute! To step down from A (4th finger on the D string), we lift off 4th finger and play G. Since open A and 4th finger on the D string are the same note. This means that stepping down from open A doesn't follow the rule! It breaks the rule! To step down from open A, we must set 3rd finger onto the D string. This is true to step down from all open strings.

3. Draw a circle on each fingerboard that steps down from the open string.

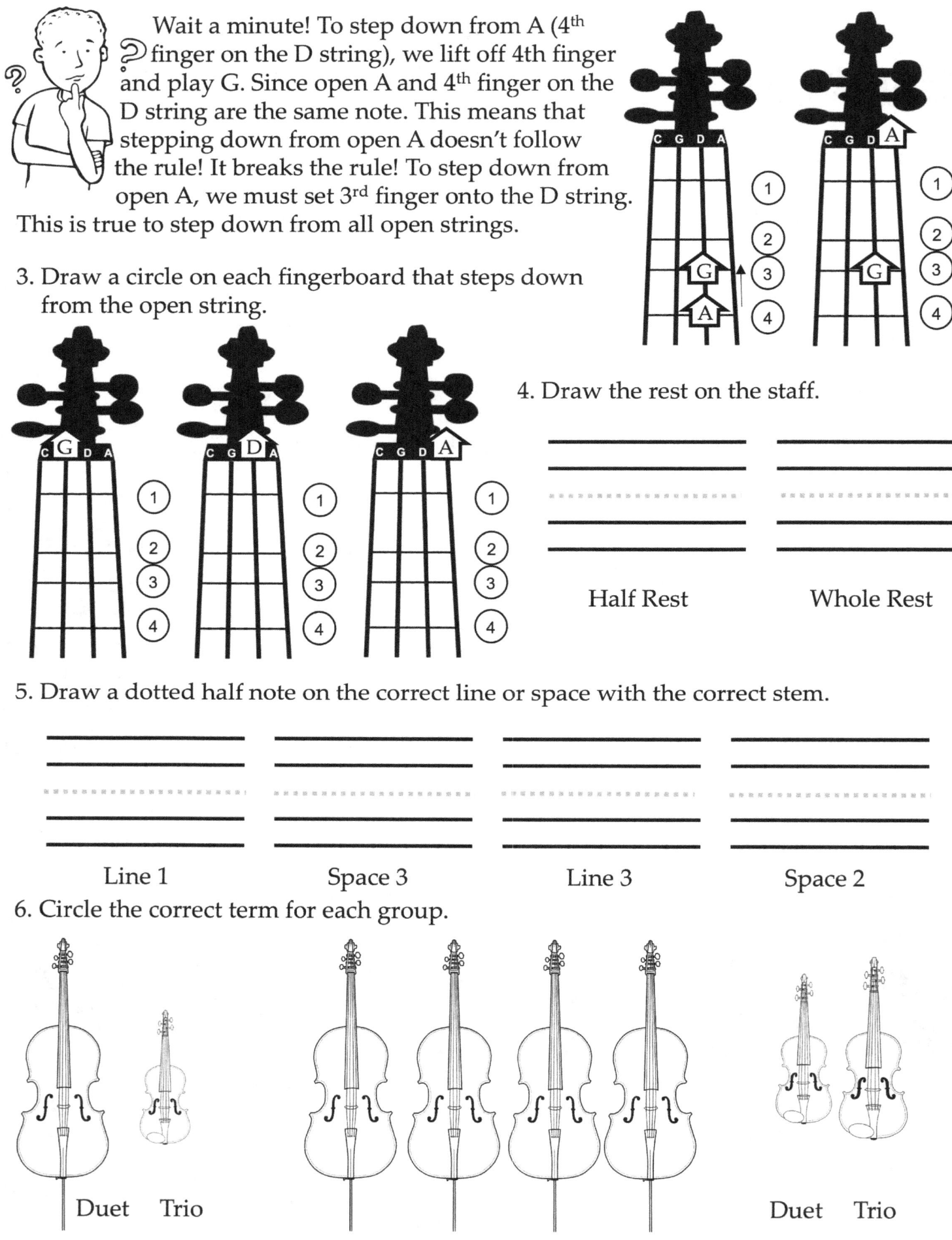

4. Draw the rest on the staff.

Half Rest   Whole Rest

5. Draw a dotted half note on the correct line or space with the correct stem.

Line 1   Space 3   Line 3   Space 2

6. Circle the correct term for each group.

Duet   Trio

Duet   Trio   Quartet

Duet   Trio

52   Quartet

Quartet

Lesson 18

1. Draw a circle stepping up on the fingerboard. Then fill in the blanks.

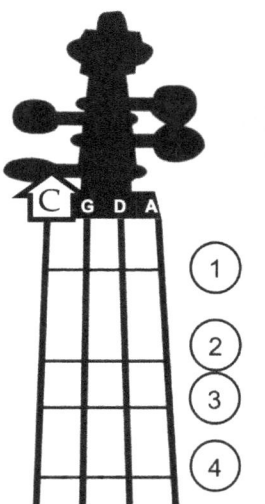

Letter: C – **step up** – land on _____

Finger: __0__ – **step up** – play finger ____.

Letter: D – **step up** – land on _____

Finger: ____ – **step up** – play finger ____.

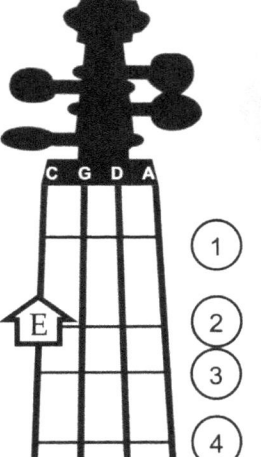

Letter: E – **step up** – land on _____

Finger: ____ – **step up** – play finger ____.

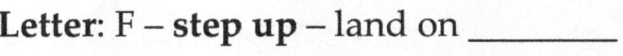

Letter: F – **step up** – land on _____

Finger: ____ – **step up** – play finger ____.

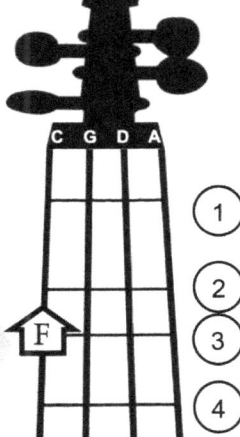

Letter: G – **step up** – land on _____

Finger: ____ – **step up** – play finger ____.

Letter: A – **step up** – land on _____

Finger: ____ – **step up** – play finger ____.

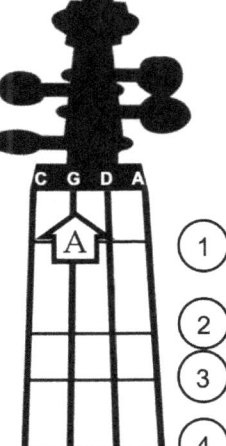

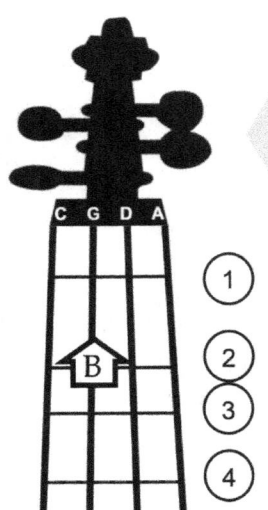

Letter: B – **step up** – land on _____

Finger: _____ – **step up** – play finger _____.

Letter: C – **step up** – land on _____

Finger: _____ – **step up** – play finger _____.

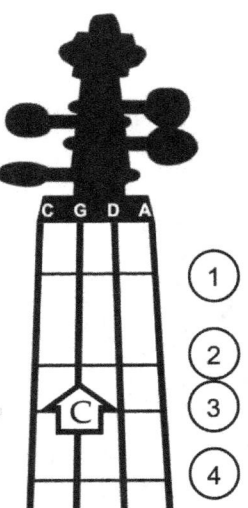

There are 2 kinds of steps, half steps and whole steps.

Half Step	Whole Step
A half step is when your fingers are **close together**. It is the closest two notes can be.	A whole step is 2 half steps together. So, there there is a **space between your fingers.**

2. On the fingerboard, color the houses yellow that are a half step apart.

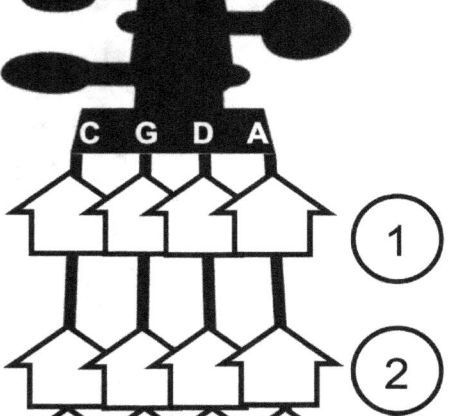

3. Look at the fingerboard on the left, circle the finger numbers that are a *whole step* apart.

1 & 2

2 & 3

3 & 4

The Magic of Music Theory Book 1 - © 2025 Horsehair Music. Photocopying prohibited.

Lesson 19

Stepping on the staff

Notes can step up and down on the staff. When a note steps up on the staff, it moves from a space to the *very next line*, or from a line to the *very next space*.

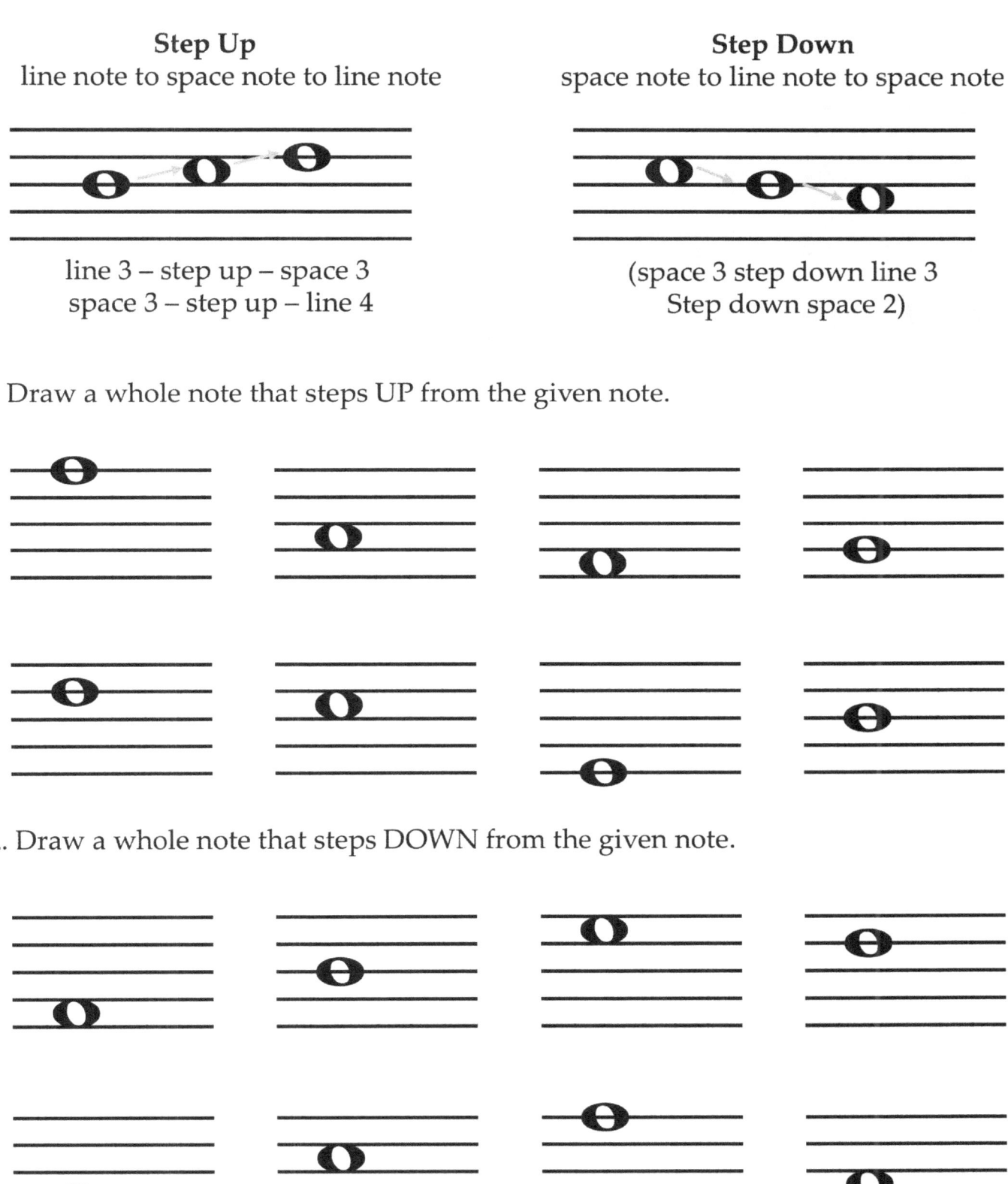

Step Up
line note to space note to line note

line 3 – step up – space 3
space 3 – step up – line 4

Step Down
space note to line note to space note

(space 3 step down line 3
Step down space 2)

1. Draw a whole note that steps UP from the given note.

2. Draw a whole note that steps DOWN from the given note.

What do you hear? #4

You will hear 3 notes. If the notes go up, color the thumbs up. If the notes stay the same, color the sideways thumb. If the notes go down, color the thumbs down.

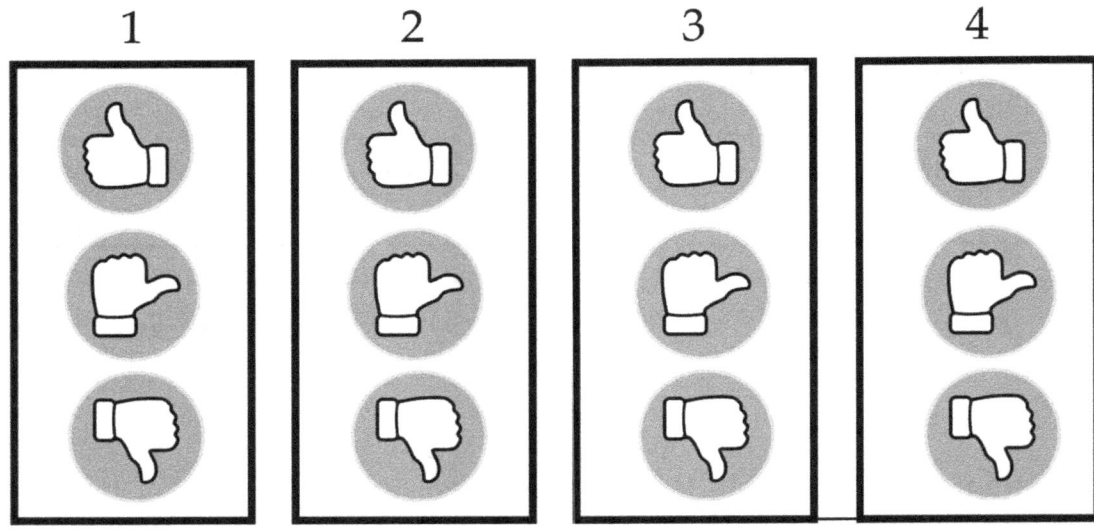

You will hear 2 melodies. If the melodies are the same, circle SAME. If the melodies are different, circle DIFFERENT.

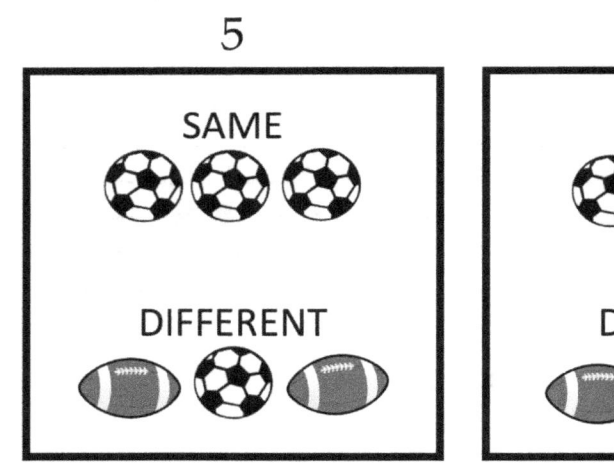
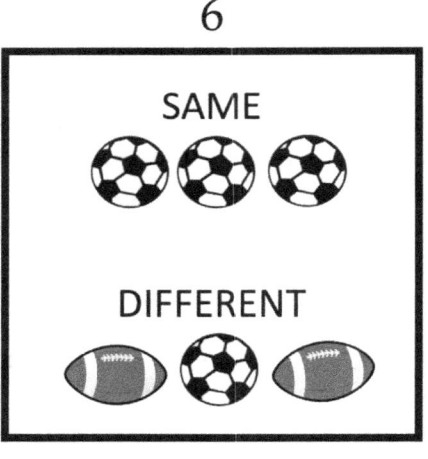
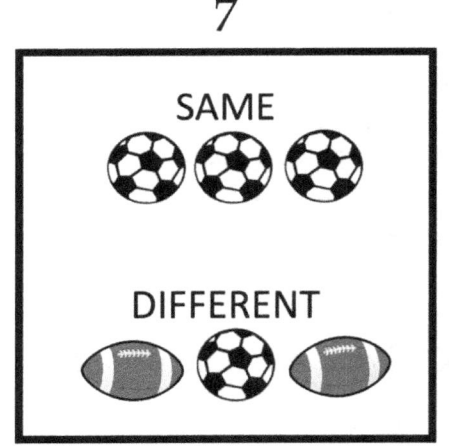

Additional ear training exercises can be found on p. 98.

Choose from these examples for questions 1-4.

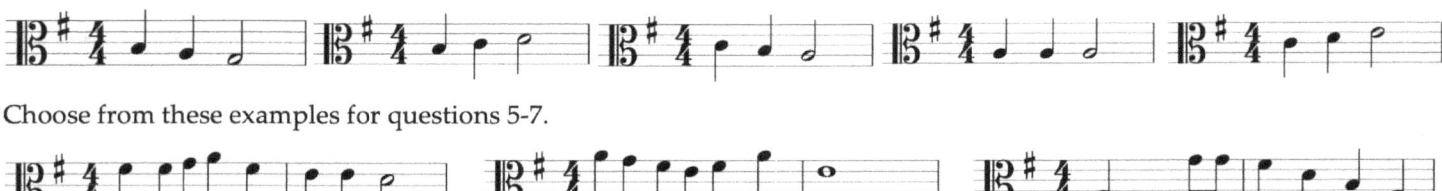

Choose from these examples for questions 5-7.

The Magic of Music Theory Book 1 - © 2025 Horsehair Music. Photocopying prohibited.

Lesson 20

1. Here are the parts of the viola and the bow. Point to each one and say its name.

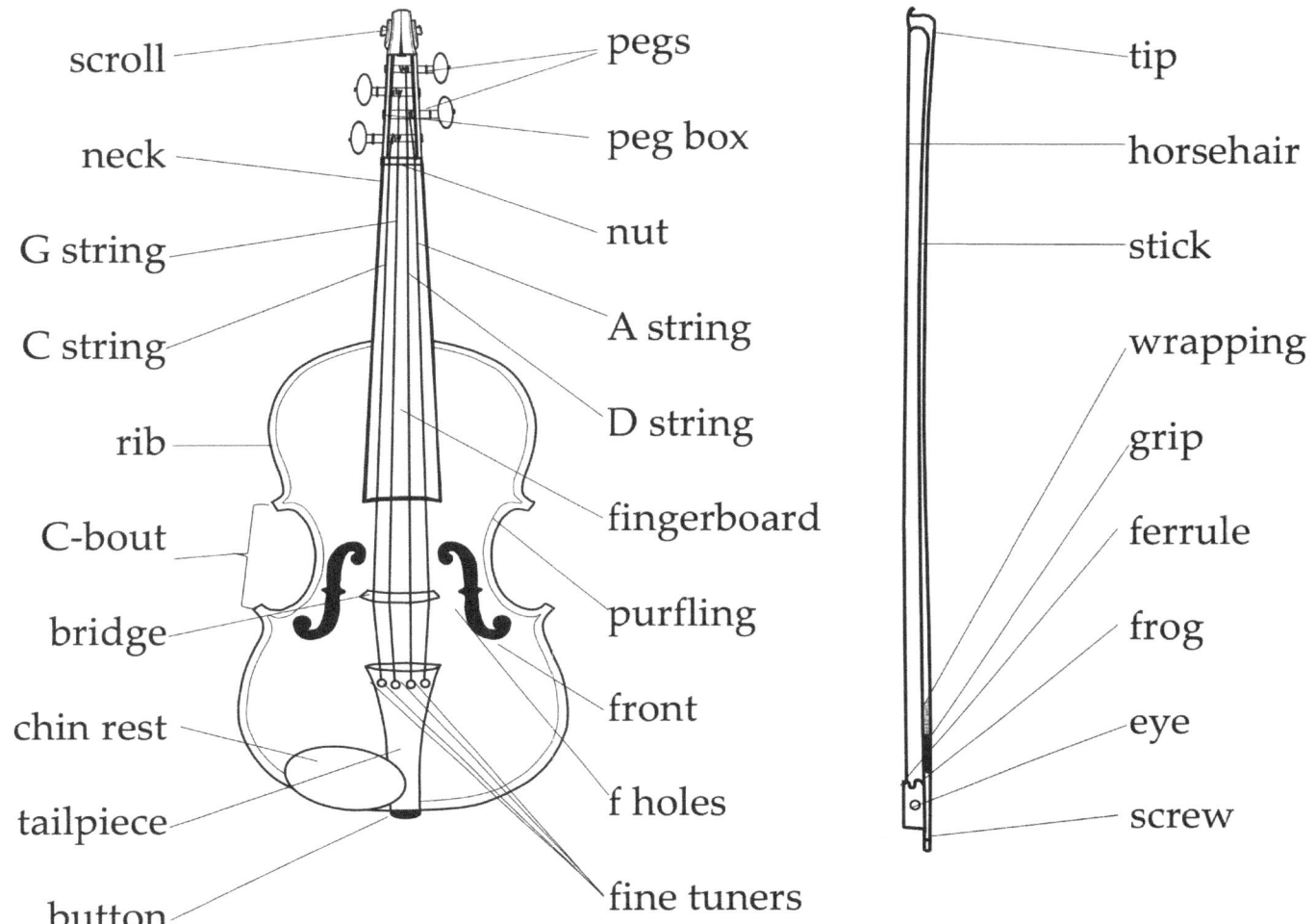

scroll
neck
G string
C string
rib
C-bout
bridge
chin rest
tailpiece
button

pegs
peg box
nut
A string
D string
fingerboard
purfling
front
f holes
fine tuners

tip
horsehair
stick
wrapping
grip
ferrule
frog
eye
screw

Did you know?
The viola is made from different kinds of wood. The top of the viola is commonly cut from spruce. The back, ribs, sides, and neck are cut out of maple. The fingerboard, tailpiece, and pegs are usually made from ebony. Ebony wood is naturally black and is strong and light. Sometimes viola makers use boxwood for the tailpiece and pegs. A person who makes stringed instruments or repairs stringed instruments is called a **luthier [loo-thee-er]**.

Stringed instruments are very old instruments. There were types of bowed instruments as early as 800 AD in Arabia, China, Spain, and France. But the first written records of luthiers are from the 1500s. Two luthiers from northern Italy, **Andrea Amati** from Cremona and **Gasparo Bertolotti** from Brescia, are some of the first known luthiers. A viola made by Andrea Amati in 1553 still exists today and is displayed at the National Music Museum in Vermillion, South Dakota.

2. Write the part of the viola in the correct box.

Scroll	Neck	A String	D String	G String
Fingerboard	Purfling	Front	Fine tuners	Chin rest
Button	Bridge	C-bout	Rib	Pegs
Nut	C String	Tailpiece	Peg Box	f holes

Lesson 21

The staff lines are divided with **bar lines** that create **measures. Bar lines** are drawn from line 5 down to line 1. Bar lines help our eyes track the notes. A bar line is drawn at the beginning of the staff. At the end of the music, you will see a **double bar line.** A **double bar line** is one thin line, and one thick line.

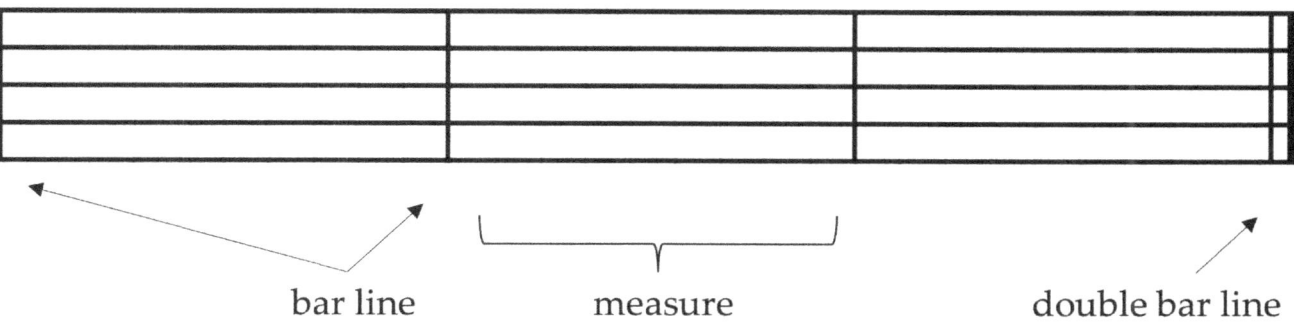

bar line   measure   double bar line

1. Divide the staff into 3 equal measures by adding bar lines and a double bar line at the end.

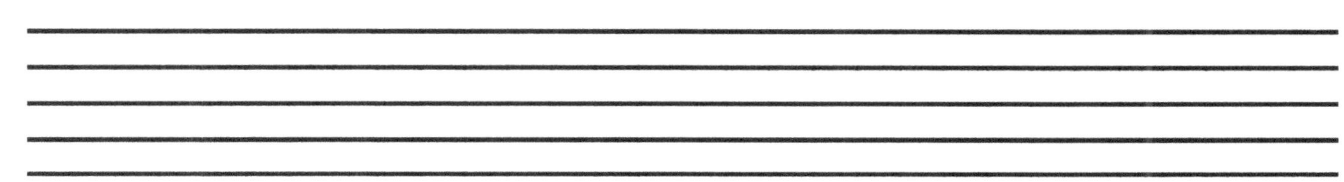

When there are dots in front of a double bar line, it is called a **repeat sign**. This symbol means go back to the beginning and play that section again.

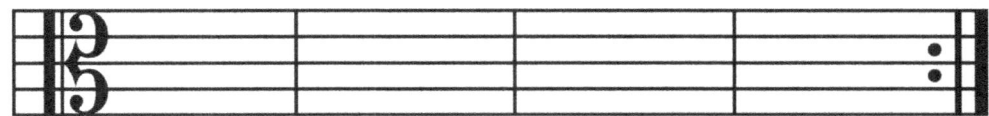

Repeat Sign

A **time signature** is two numbers stacked on top of each other. A time signature is written at the beginning of a piece. It is printed on the right side next to the clef. The top number is between lines 3 and 5, and the bottom number is between lines 1 and 3.

The top number tells us how many beats are in each measure. The bottom number tells us what kind of note gets one beat. *A 4 on the bottom means the quarter note gets 1 beat.*

2. Circle the top number of the time signatures. Draw a box around the bottom number.

$\frac{3}{4}$ $\frac{5}{4}$ $\frac{4}{4}$ $\frac{2}{4}$ $\frac{6}{4}$

59

3. Write the correct top number of each time signature in the box.

4. Add the missing bar lines. Do not draw your bar line outside of the staff. A bar line can not extend below line 1 or past line 5. Don't forget the double bar line at the end!

5. Draw a line from the dog to the water bowl that matches the number of beats.

The number of beats in each measure should add up to the top number of the time signature. We count the number of beats in each measure.

6. Write the number of beats for the note in each heart. Write the counts for each measure on the lines. The first line is done for you.

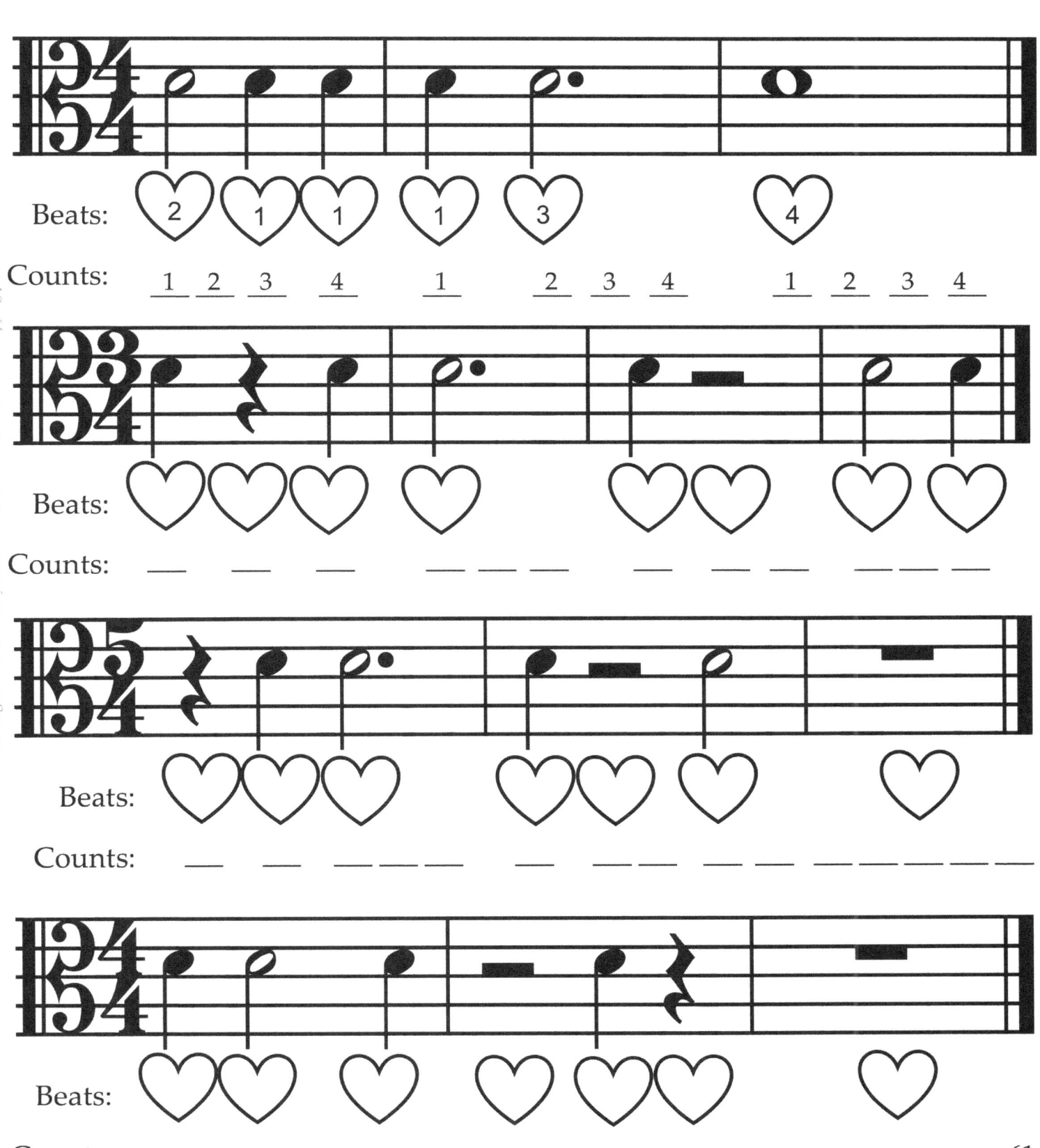

61

What do you hear? #5

You will hear 1 of the rhythms in each box. Circle the rhythm you hear.

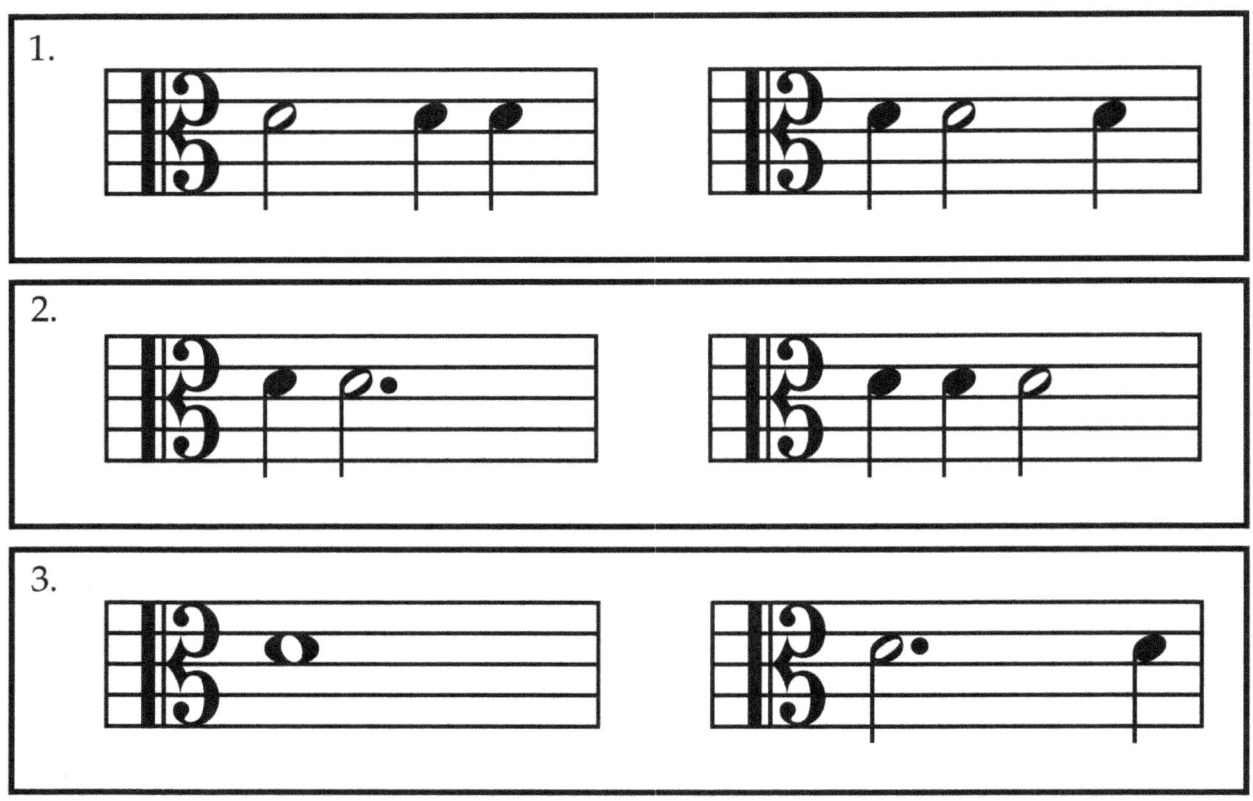

If the example you hear is fast, color the sports car; if it is slow, color the bus.

 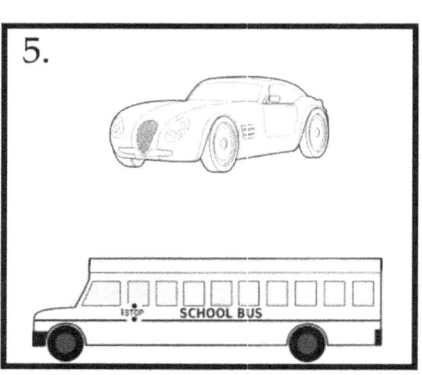 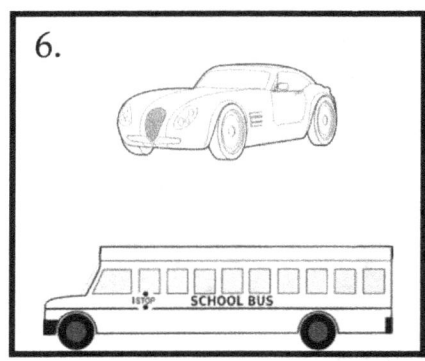

* Additional ear training exercises can be found on pp. 100 & 101.

Choose one example from each box for questions 1 - 3.

Choose one example below for questions 4 – 6 and exaggerate the tempo.

Remo Giazotto – Albinoni's Adagio in G Minor

Giochino Rossini – William Tell Overture

Antonio Vivaldi – "The Four Seasons," Summer, III. Presto

Johann Sebastian Bach – Air

The Magic of Music Theory Book 1 - © 2025 Horsehair Music. Photocopying prohibited.

Lesson 22

1. Draw an alto clef on each staff and the correct G string note.

Open G	A	B	C
Quarter Note	Half Note	Dotted Half Note	Quarter Note

2. Draw an alto clef on each staff and the correct D string note.

Open D	E	F#	G
Half Note	Dotted Half Note	Whole note	Quarter Note

3. Draw an alto clef on each staff and the correct C string note.

Open C	D	E	F
Whole Note	Quarter Note	Dotted Half Note	Half Note

4. Draw an alto clef on each staff and the correct A string note.

Open A	B	C#	G
Quarter Note	Half Note	Whole Note	Dotted Half Note

Compose a tune using the notes on the D string following the steps.

1. Clap and count the rhythm.
2. Clap and say the words.
3. The first and last notes are given to you. We will start and end on D.
   Choose only from the D string. Write one letter in each circle.
4. Listen to your teacher play your new song.
5. You try playing your new song.

Hey Diddle Diddle

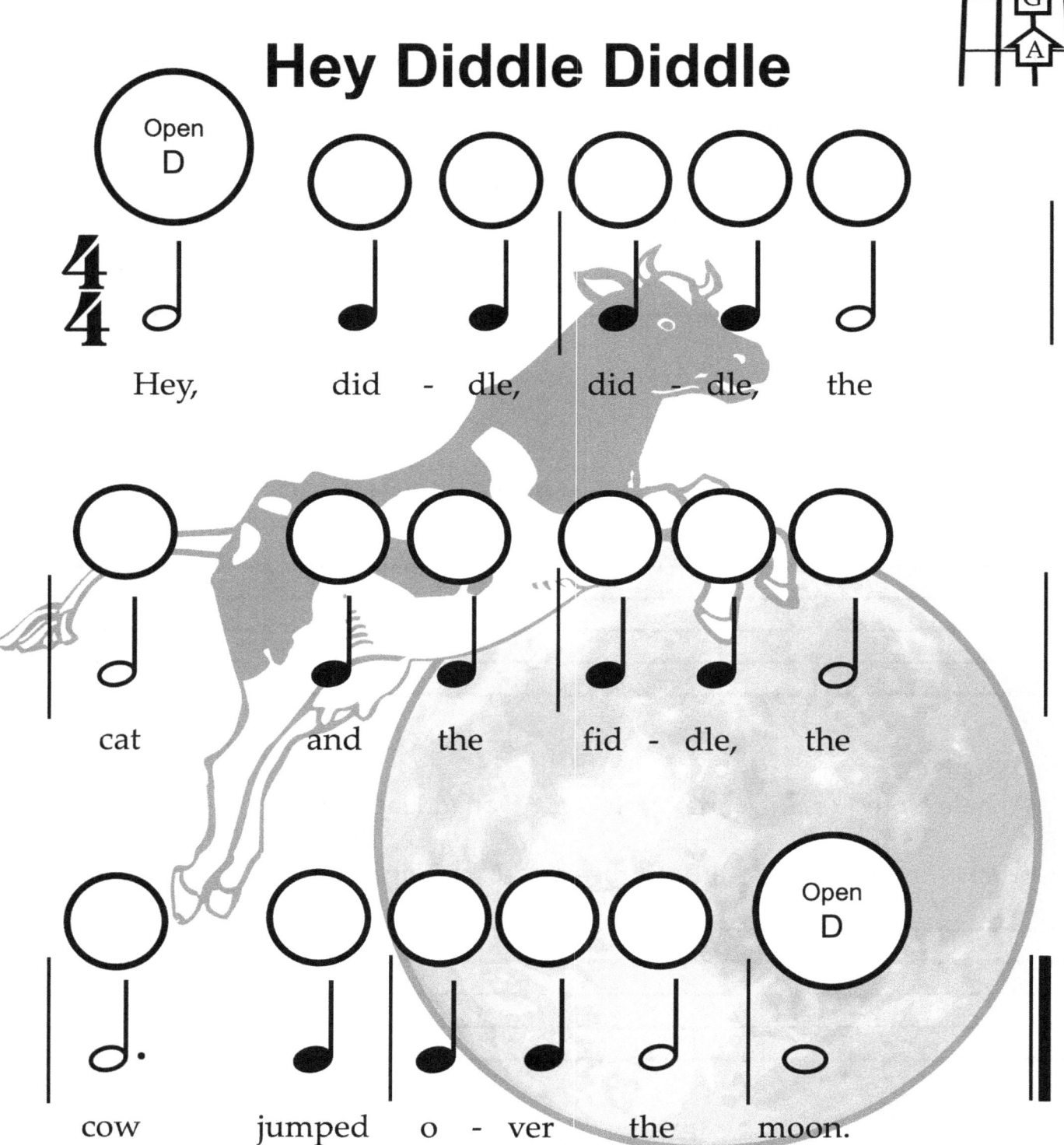

The Magic of Music Theory Book 1 - © 2025 Horsehair Music. Photocopying prohibited.

What do you hear? #6

Circle the name of the string you hear.

1.	2.	3.	4.
C G D A	C G D A	C G D A	C G D A

Circle the dynamic you hear.

5.	6.	7.
f *mf* *p*	*f* *mf* *p*	*f* *mf* *p*

Circle the rhythm you hear.

8.
 or

9.
 or

* Additional ear training exercises can be found on pp. 96, 97 & 100

Choose one example for questions 1-4.

Choose one example for questions 5-7 and exaggerate the dynamic.

Alexander Borodin – Prince Igor   Ludwig van Beethoven – Minuet in G

Peter Ilych Tchaikovsky – 1812 Overture

Choose one example in each box for questions 8 & 9.

Lesson 23

1. Draw a stem on each note head to make quarter notes.

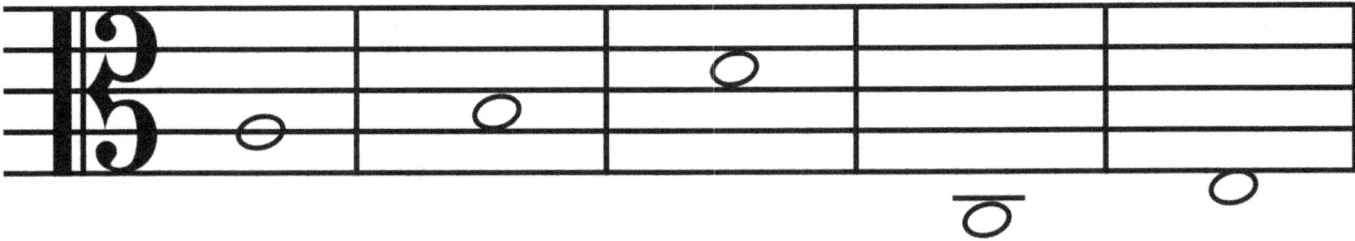

2. Draw a stem on each note head below to make half notes.

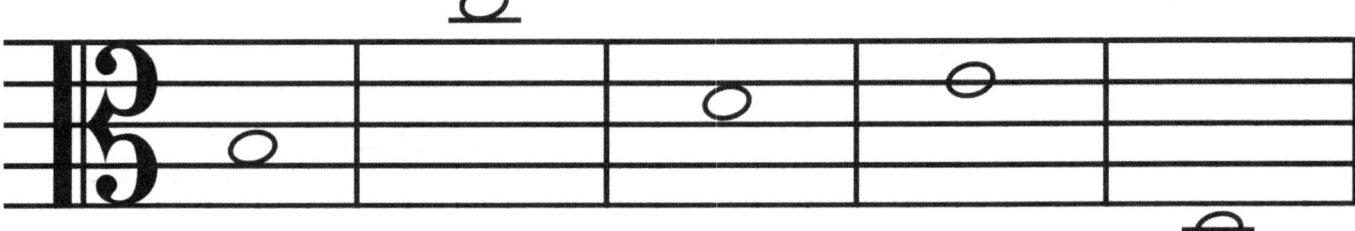

3. Draw a stem and add a dot to each note head below to make dotted half notes.

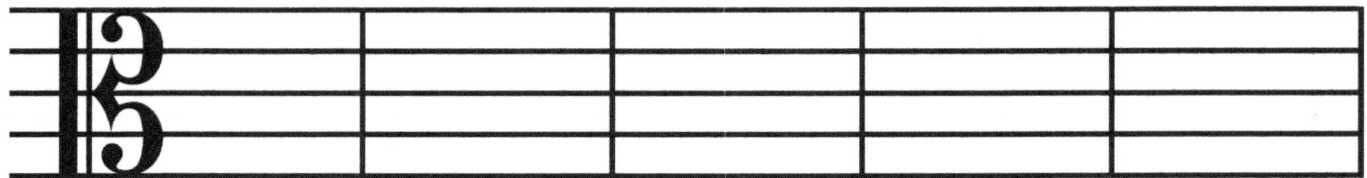

4. Draw the note on the staff. Remember the stem and dot rules!

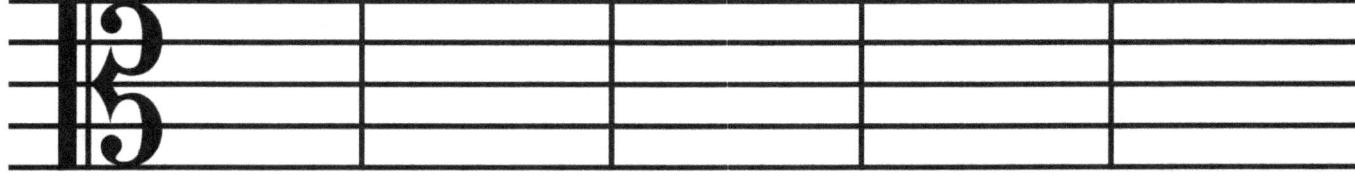

A	D	C#	F#	E
Half Note	Quarter Note	Whole Note	Dotted Half Note	Whole Note

F#	G	A	C	D
Half Note	Quarter Note	Whole Note	Dotted Half Note	Whole Note

The Magic of Music Theory Book 1 - © 2025 Horsehair Music. Photocopying prohibited.

5. Write the number of beats in the hearts. Write the counts for each measure on the lines.

Beats:

Counts: ___ ___ ___ ___   ___ ___ ___

Beats:

Counts: ___ ___ ___ ___   ___   ___

Beats:

Counts: ___ ___ ___ ___   ___ ___   ___ ___

Beats:

Counts: ___ ___ ___ ___   ___ ___ ___   ___ ___ ___

6. Write the name of each symbol on the line.

mf

_____   _____

mp

_____   _____

Lesson 24

One day as Jess and McKinley were waiting for the school bus, they realized they were a little bit hungry. Jess looked inside her backpack and found a snack her mom had packed for her. When she looked in the bag she found 1 banana, 1 cookie, and 1 jelly sandwich. But there was only one of each thing in the bag! What should she do? She knew McKinley was hungry too and she didn't want to eat when her friend didn't have a snack. Suddenly she had an idea! She could split each snack in half. Then they could both share all the snacks!

So, Jess took the banana and split it in half. Now the *one* banana was in *two* pieces. She took the sandwich out of the bag and realized her mom had cut it in half! Perfect! Jess took the *one sandwich* and gave one half to McKinley, and she kept the other half! Then she took the *one* cookie and split it into *two* pieces. She got half of the cookie, and McKinley got half of the cookie. In music class that day they learned that *one* quarter note can be split in half, and it becomes *two* notes, called **eighth notes.** Two eighth notes together **share** one beat. Each eighth note gets ½ of a beat.

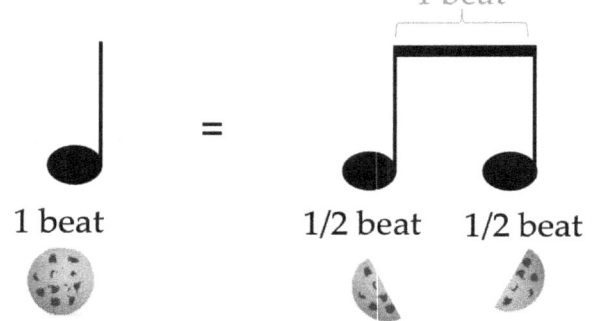

The line that connects the stems and makes 2 eighth notes is called a **beam**.

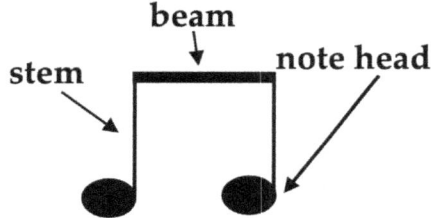

1. Trace the eighth notes and color in the note heads.

2 - eighths	2 - eighths	1	and	1	and
(clap - clap)	(clap - clap)	(clap)	(clap)	(clap)	(clap)

2. Clap and say their name, "2 eighths." (Clap for each note that you see.)
3. Clap and say their beats. To show that the 2 eighths share 1 beat, clap and say "1" on the first eighth note. Then, clap and say "and" on the second eighth note.

The Magic of Music Theory Book 1 - © 2025 Horsehair Music. Photocopying prohibited.

Follow the code and color the picture

1 Beat – Green
2 Beats – Yellow
3 Beats – Red
4 Beats – Purple
Alto Clef – Orange
Staff – Blue

Lesson 25

A **scale** is made up of 8 notes. It follows a pattern of whole steps (Whole or W) and half steps (Half or H). The major scale is built using this pattern:

Begin	Whole	Whole	Half	Whole	Whole	Whole	Half
	(W)	(W)	(H)	(W)	(W)	(W)	(H)

1. Write the first letter of the whole and half step pattern below.

Begin ____ ____ ____ ____ ____ ____ ____

Choose a silly sentence to help you remember the order:
- We Worked Hard When We Worked Hard.
- Willy Wonka Had Wee Willi Winky Honk.
- Wally Won't Help When Whitney Won't Help.

ALWAYS step up to the next letter in the alphabet when building a scale.

2. Look at the fingerboard and fill in the blanks for the D Major Scale.

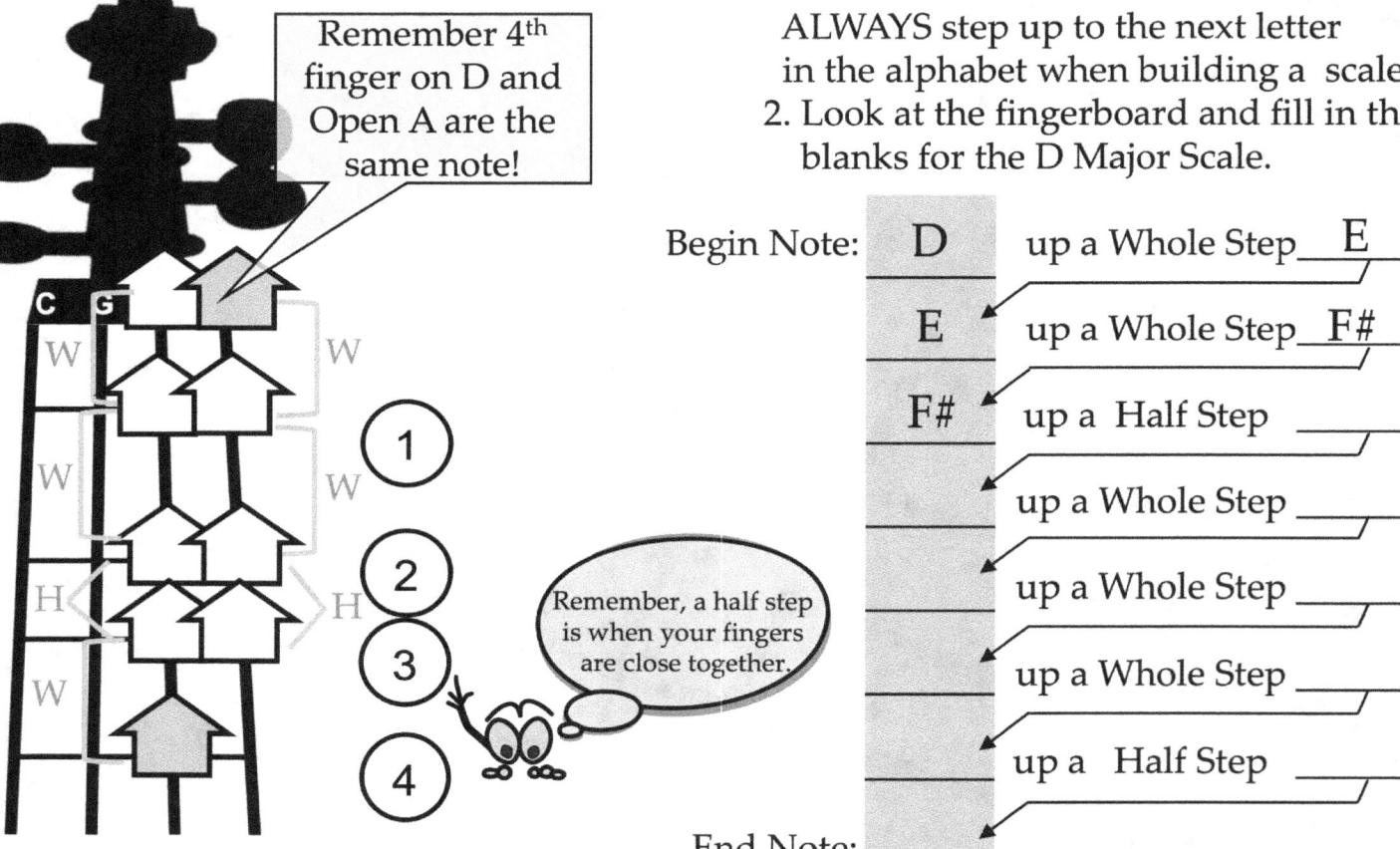

Remember 4th finger on D and Open A are the same note!

Remember, a half step is when your fingers are close together.

Begin Note:	D	up a Whole Step	E
	E	up a Whole Step	F#
	F#	up a Half Step	____
	____	up a Whole Step	____
	____	up a Whole Step	____
	____	up a Whole Step	____
	____	up a Half Step	____
End Note:	____		

3. Using the letters in the gray box, write the notes for the D major scale on the staff using whole notes. (Remember, sharps go on the left side of the note head.)

4. Write the first letter of the whole and half step pattern for a major scale.

Begin _____   _____   _____   _____   _____   _____   _____

5. Fill in the blanks for the G Major Scale.

Remember 4th finger on G and Open D are the same note!

C   A

①
②
③
④

Begin Note: **G**   up a Whole Step _____

up a Whole Step _____

up a Half Step _____

up a Whole Step _____

up a Whole Step _____

up a Whole Step _____

up a   Half Step _____

End Note: _____

This is the same letter as the begin note, but it sounds higher!

6. Look at the gray column in #5 and draw the G scale on the staff using whole notes.

7. Write the number of beats in the hearts. Write the counts on the lines.

Beats: ♡   ♡   ♡   ♡   ♡

Counts: _ _ _ _ _ _ _ _ _

Lesson 26

1. Write the whole and half step pattern for the major scale.

Begin _____ _____ _____ _____ _____ _____ _____

2. Fill in the blanks for the C major scale.

The first note is called the **keynote** or **tonic**

Remember 4th finger on C and Open G are the same note!

A   E

① 1

② 2

③ 3

④ 4

Begin Note: C   up a Whole Step _____

up a Whole Step _____

up a Half Step _____

up a Whole Step _____

up a Whole Step _____

up a Whole Step _____

up a Half Step _____

End Note: _____

The Magic of Music Theory Book 1 - © 2025 Horsehair Music. Photocopying prohibited.

3. Look at the gray column in #2 and write the C scale on the staff using whole notes.

Circle the answer.

4. When I play the C scale, to play G I use: 4th FINGER   THE OPEN G STRING

5. The first note of the scale is called: STARTING LINE   TONIC   TREBLE

Each piece you play is based on a scale. A composer chooses notes from the scale to write a composition. Often, a composer will start or end a piece on the **keynote/tonic.**

6. Compose a piece. Begin and end your composition on the tonic. Choose only notes that are in the G Major scale to write in the circles.

Title:_____

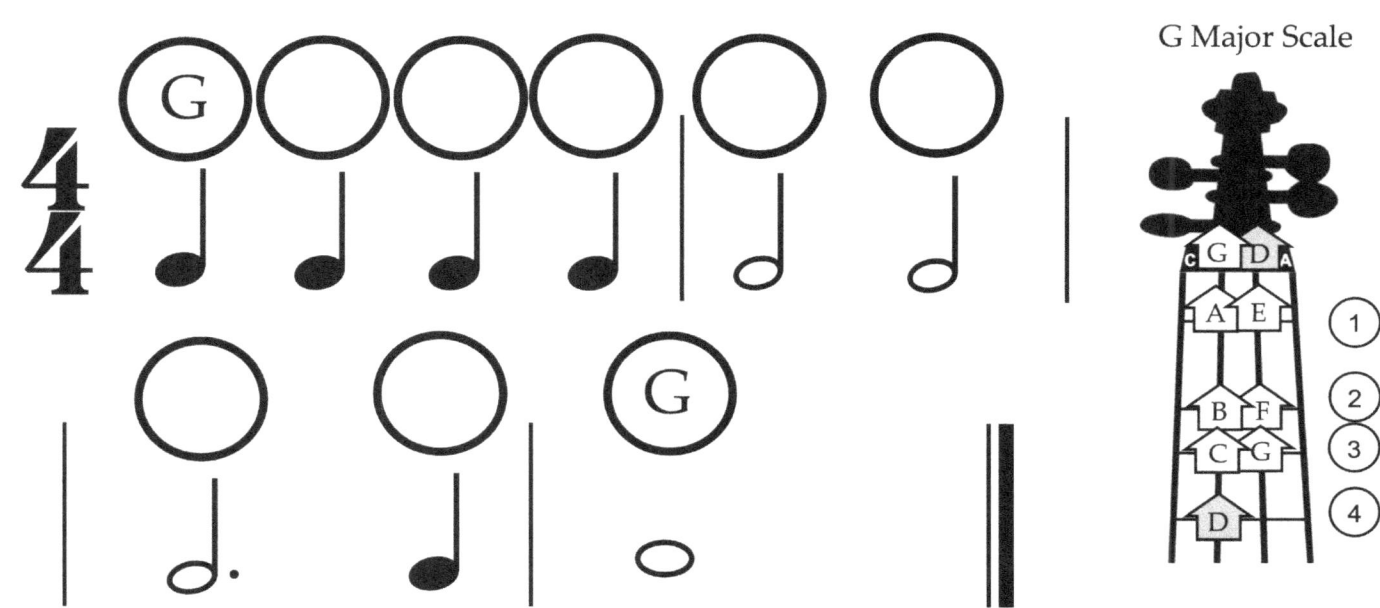

7. Try playing your composition or ask your teacher to play it for you.

8. Write the number of beats in the hearts. Write the counts on the lines.

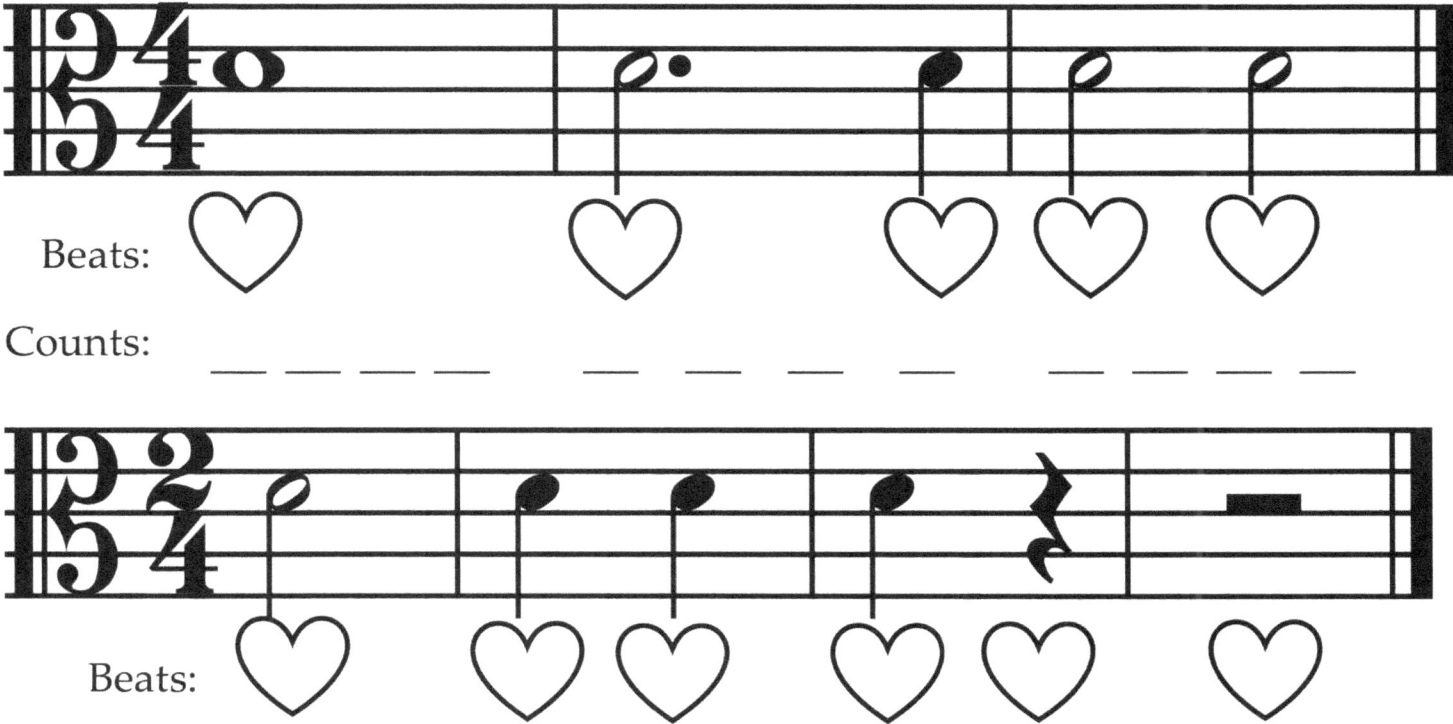

Beats:

Counts:

Lesson 27

1. Write the letter name of each note in the blank.

____ ____ ____ ____ ____

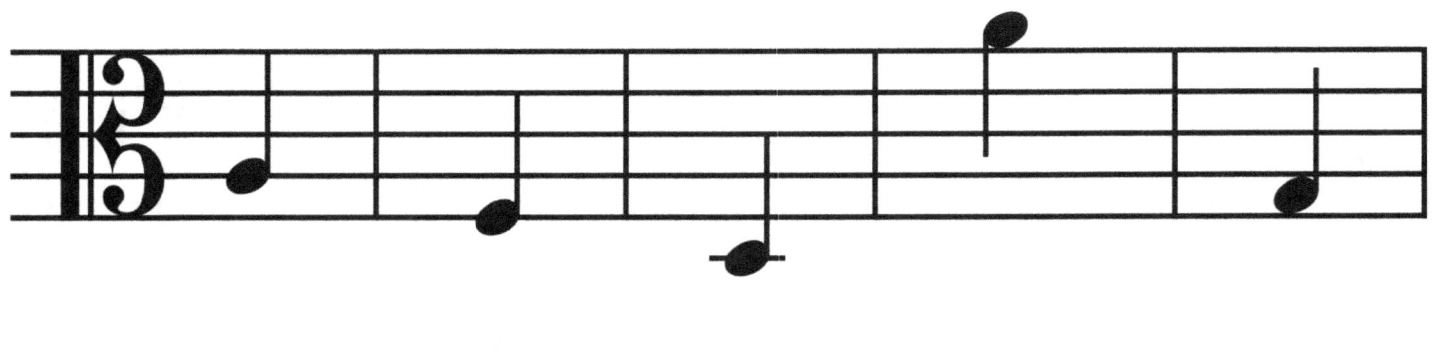

____ ____ ____ ____ ____

2. Write the number of beats in each heart.

3. Write the term on the line that the arrow is pointing to. (beam, note head, stem)

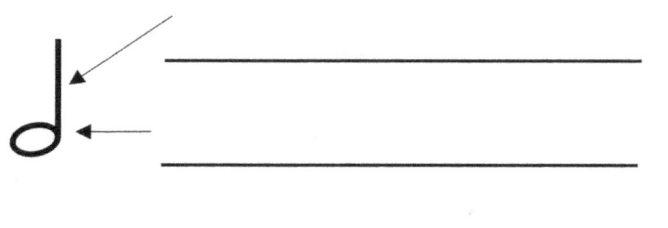

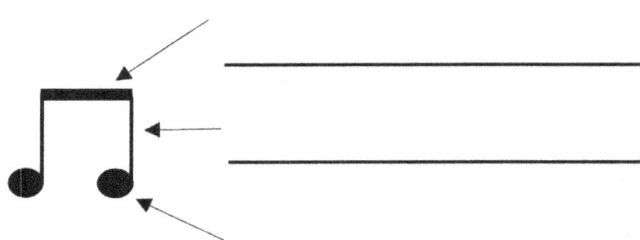

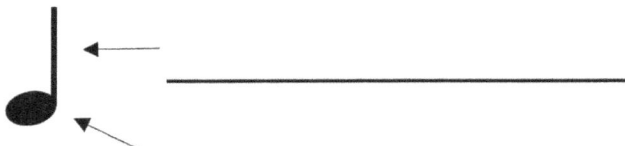

4. Draw an X through the incorrect scale patterns and circle the correct patterns.

Begin W W H W W W H   Begin W W H W H W H

Begin W W H W W W H   Begin W H W W W W H

Begin W H W H W W H   Begin W W H W W W H

5. Color the houses that are used in each scale. The keynote (first note you color) is listed under each fingerboard.

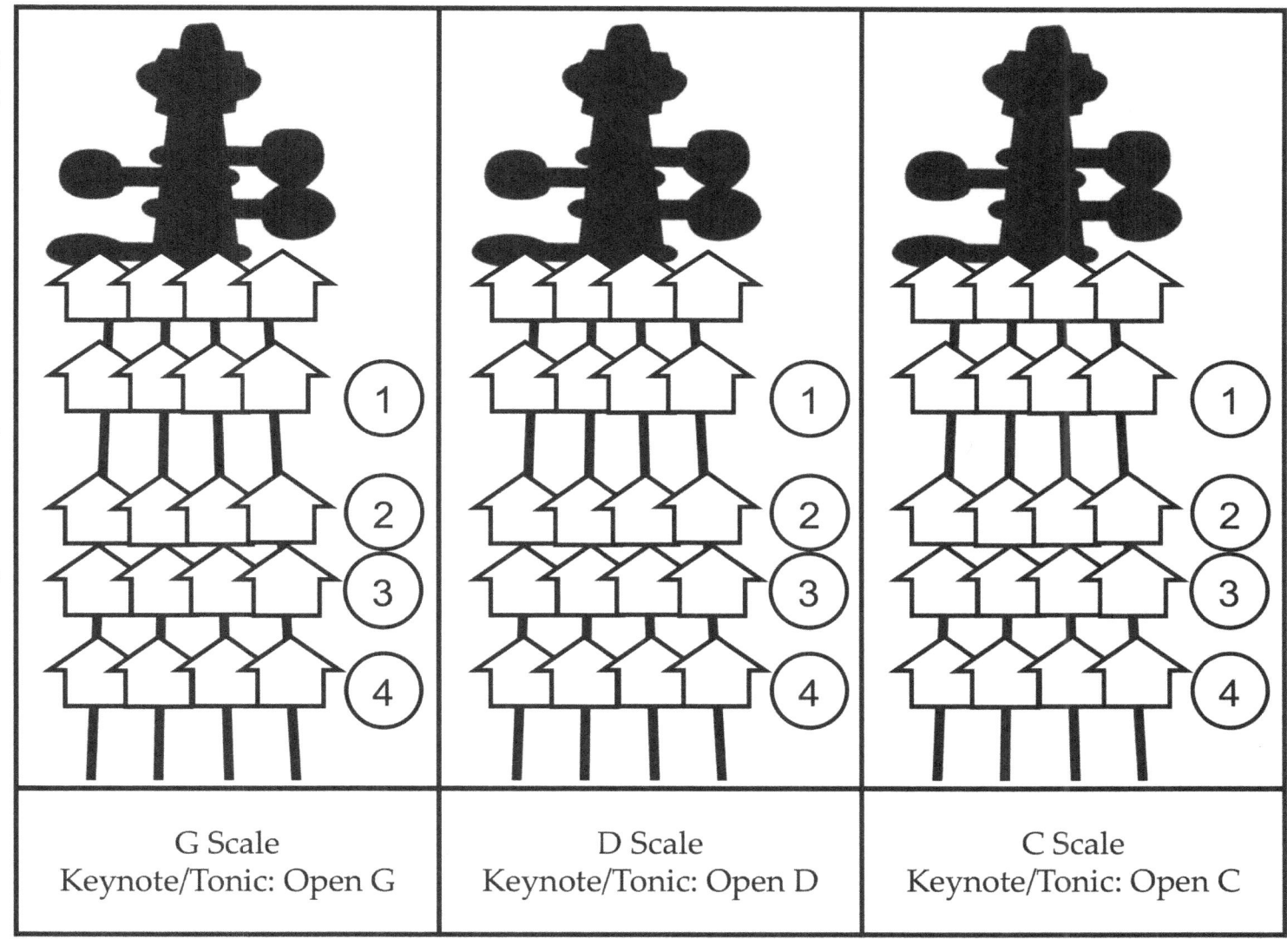

| G Scale Keynote/Tonic: Open G | D Scale Keynote/Tonic: Open D | C Scale Keynote/Tonic: Open C |

6. What is the 5th note of the G scale? _____

7. What is the 5th note of the D scale? _____

8. What is the 5th note of the A scale? _____

(Hint: Count the first house in the scale as "1")

What do you hear? #7

Circle if the notes you hear are stepping up, stepping down, or repeating.

| Stepping up | Stepping down | Repeating |

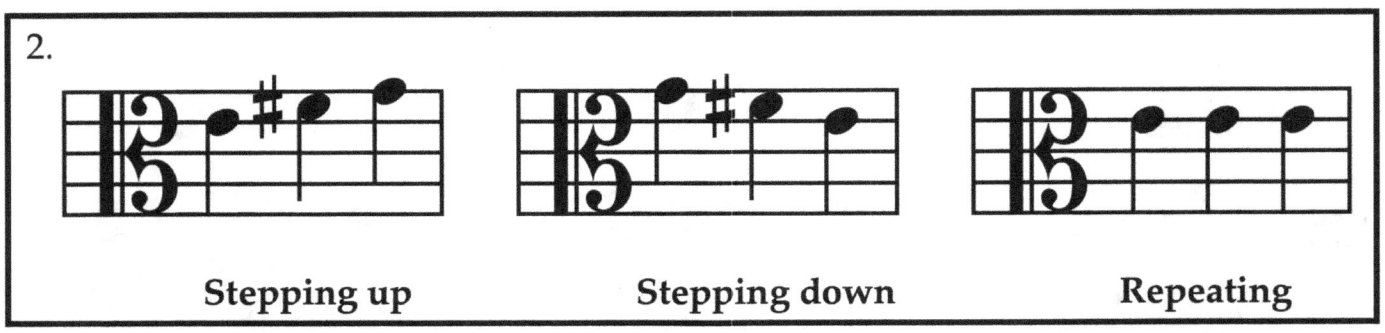

| Stepping up | Stepping down | Repeating |

| Stepping up | Stepping down | Repeating |

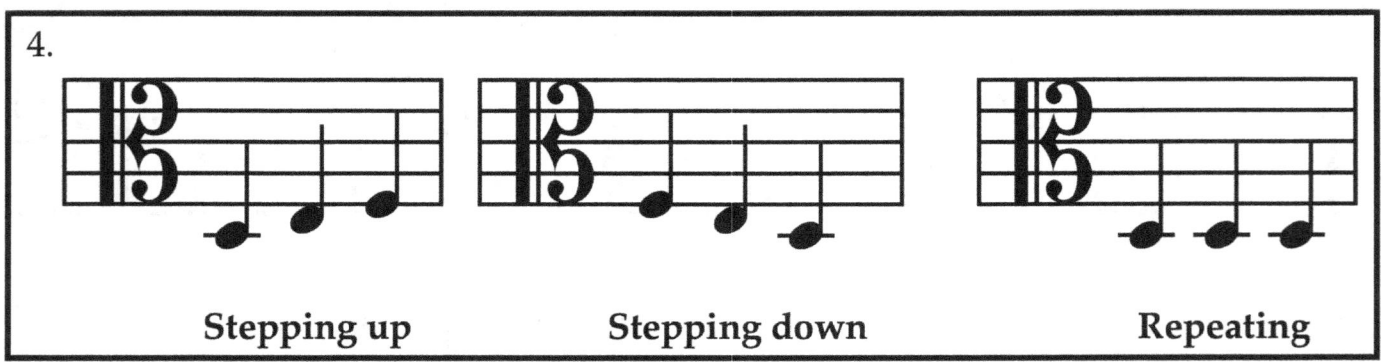

| Stepping up | Stepping down | Repeating |

* Additional ear training exercises can be found on p. 98

Choose one of the examples in each box to play.

The Magic of Music Theory Book 1 - © 2025 Horsehair Music. Photocopying prohibited.

Lesson 28

When we walk up stairs, sometimes it is fun to take a giant step and skip a step. We can skip up in the music alphabet too. Start on one letter skip a letter, land on the next letter. We can skip up or down through the music alphabet. To skip down, skip backwards through the music alphabet.

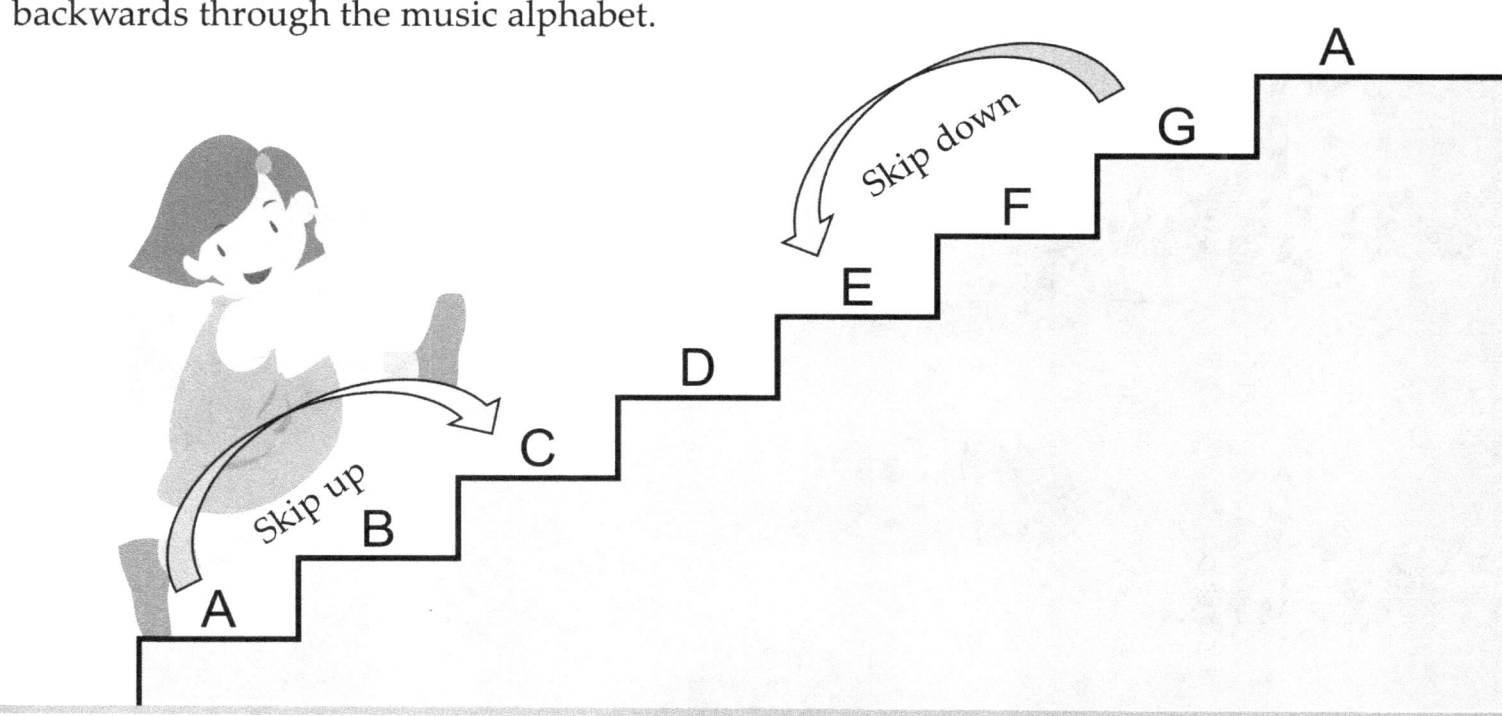

1. Fill in the missing letters. The first one is done for you

Skipping Up	
A (skip __B__) land on __C__	E (skip _____) land on _____
B (skip _____) land on _____	F (skip _____) land on _____
C (skip _____) land on _____	G (skip _____) land on _____
D (skip _____) land on _____	A (skip _____) land on _____

Skipping Down	
A (skip _____) land on _____	E (skip _____) land on _____
B (skip _____) land on _____	F (skip _____) land on _____
C (skip _____) land on _____	G (skip _____) land on _____
D (skip _____) land on _____	A (skip _____) land on _____

Step & Skip

Molly the mole is bored! So, she decided to entertain herself by practicing skips and steps. Help Molly play her game. Place a coin or little toy on Molly's dirt pile. Roll a die. and move the coin or toy according the numbers.

Roll 1 = stay on that letter, Roll 2 = step up, Roll 3 = skip up, Roll 4, 5 or 6 = roll again.

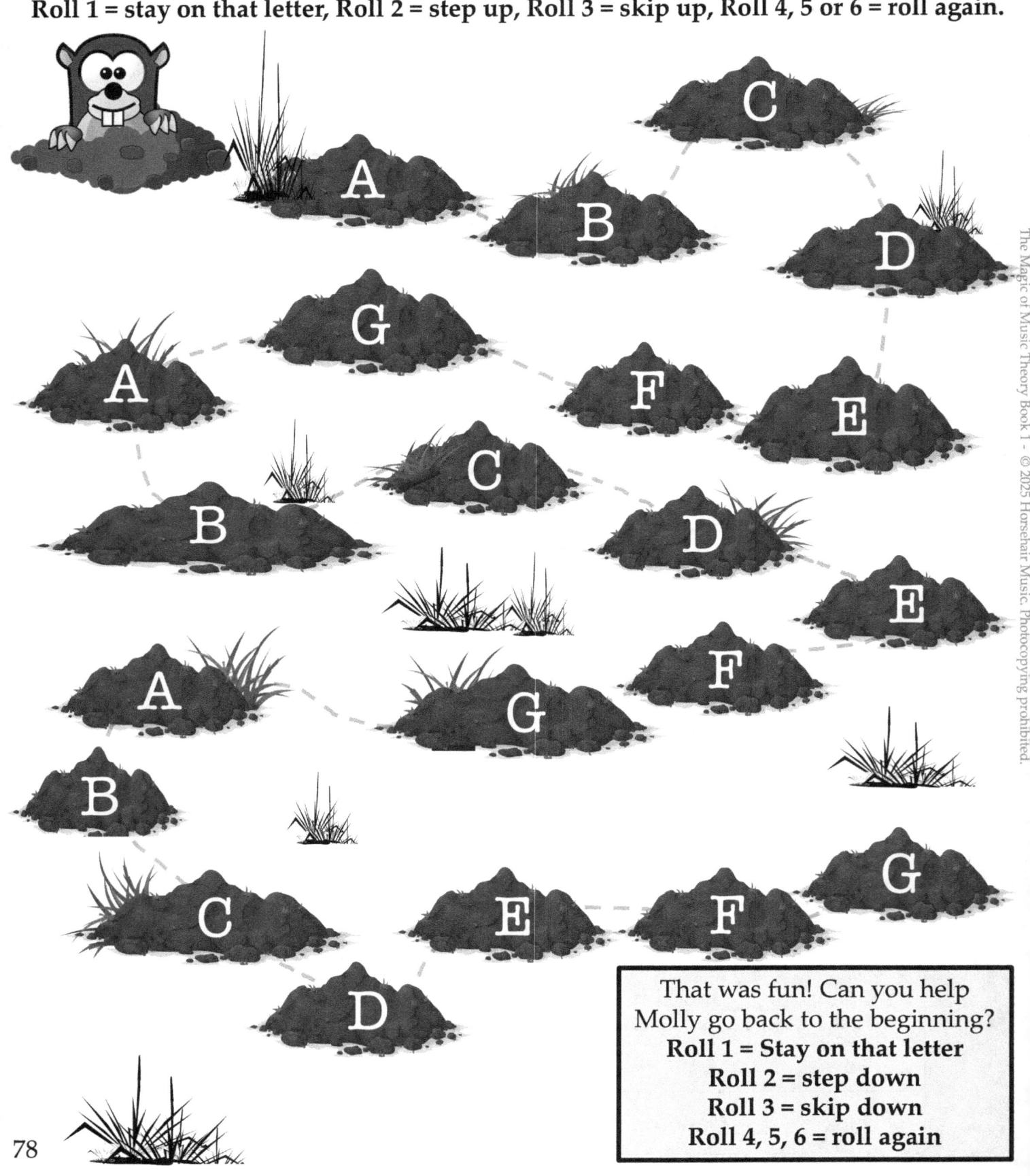

That was fun! Can you help
Molly go back to the beginning?
**Roll 1 = Stay on that letter
Roll 2 = step down
Roll 3 = skip down
Roll 4, 5, 6 = roll again**

Discover the Composers

Fill in the letter name to learn about the life of a great composer while you listen to Vivaldi's Concerto No. 2 in G Minor, Op. 8, III. Presto, RV 315.

Antonio Viv___l___i was born in Venice. Vivaldi had r___ ___

h___ir. Since he was a priest, His ni___kname was "the R___d Priest.

He t___u___ht violin at an orph___n ___ ___ ___ for girls. He wrote

ov___r 200 ___on___ ___rtos. His most ___ ___mous concertos

are ___ ___ ll___ ___ the "___our S___ ___sons" and Vivaldi makes

the violin sound like ___i___ ___ ___rent thin___s in n___tur___.

Lesson 29

Skip Up

To **skip up** on the fingerboard, skip one finger (one letter). Remember, 4th finger, and the next open string are the same note.

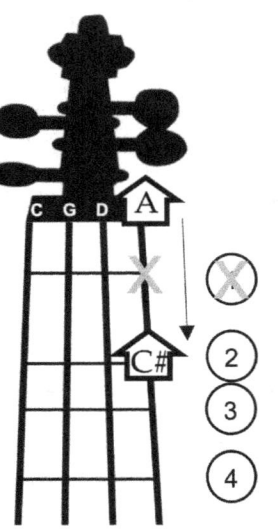

Skip Down

To **skip down** on the fingerboard, lift 2 fingers up. Remember, you might have to set fingers down on the next string to the left.

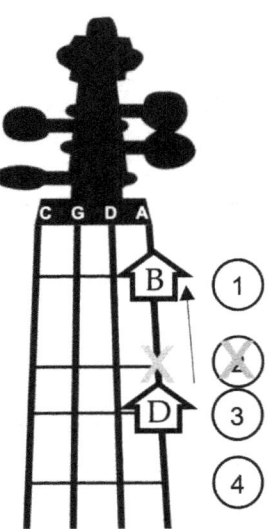

1. Draw a circle on the fingerboard showing a skip up.

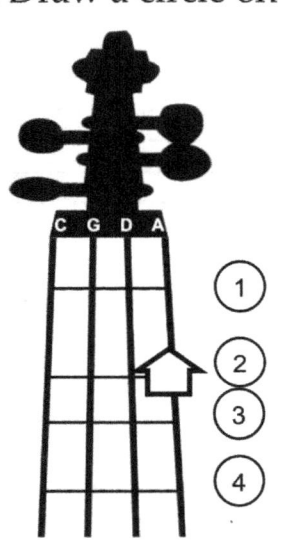 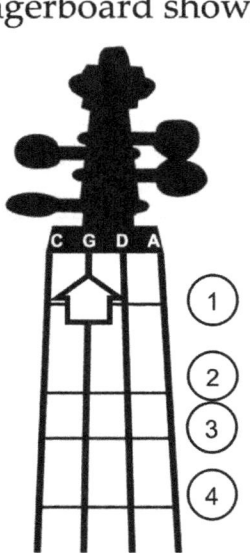 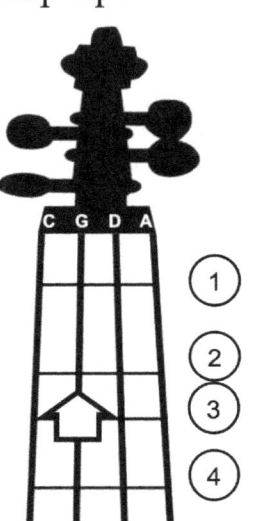 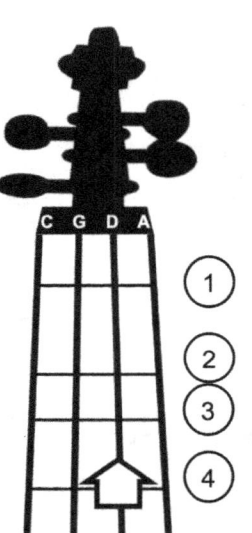

2. Draw a circle on the fingerboard showing a skip down.

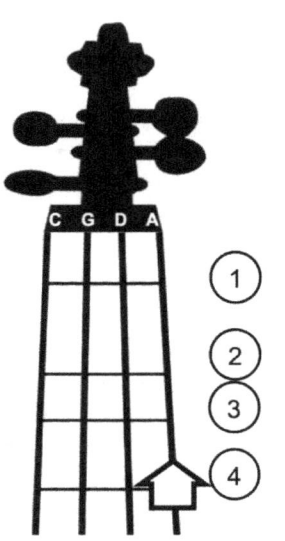 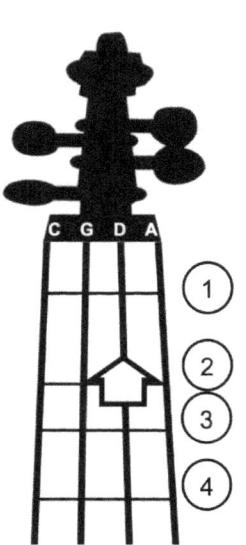 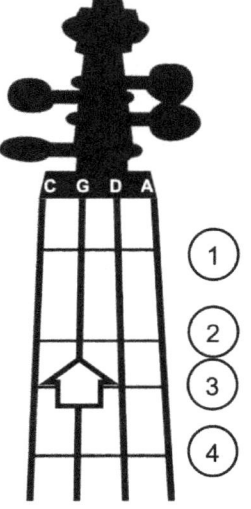 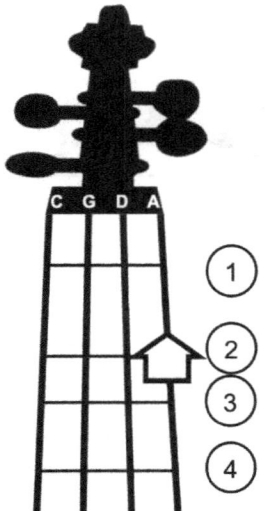

80

Skipping on the staff

Notes can skip up and down on the staff. When a note skips up on the staff, it moves from a line to the very next line (and skips the space) or it moves from a space to the very next space (and skips the line).

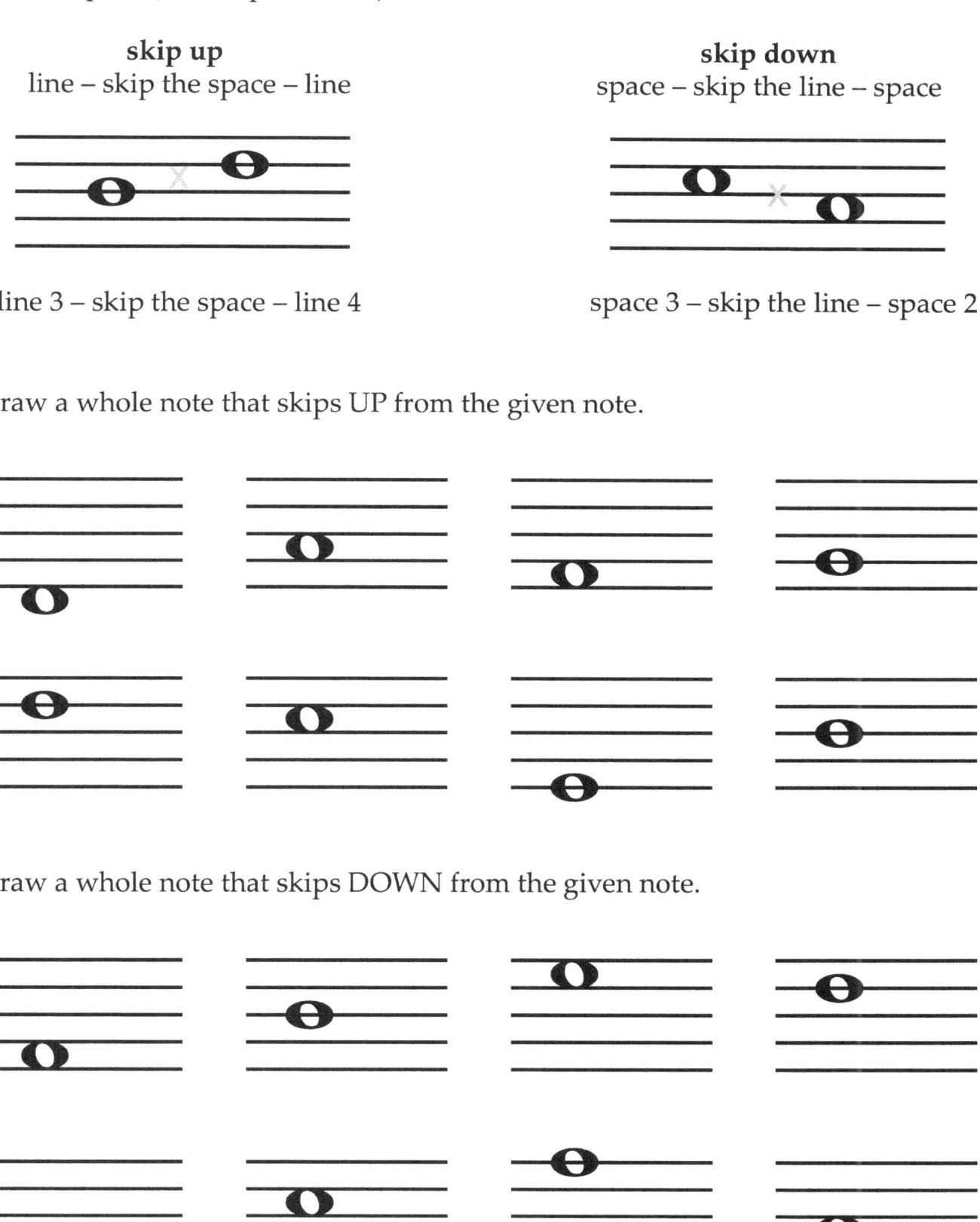

skip up
line – skip the space – line

line 3 – skip the space – line 4

skip down
space – skip the line – space

space 3 – skip the line – space 2

3. Draw a whole note that skips UP from the given note.

4. Draw a whole note that skips DOWN from the given note.

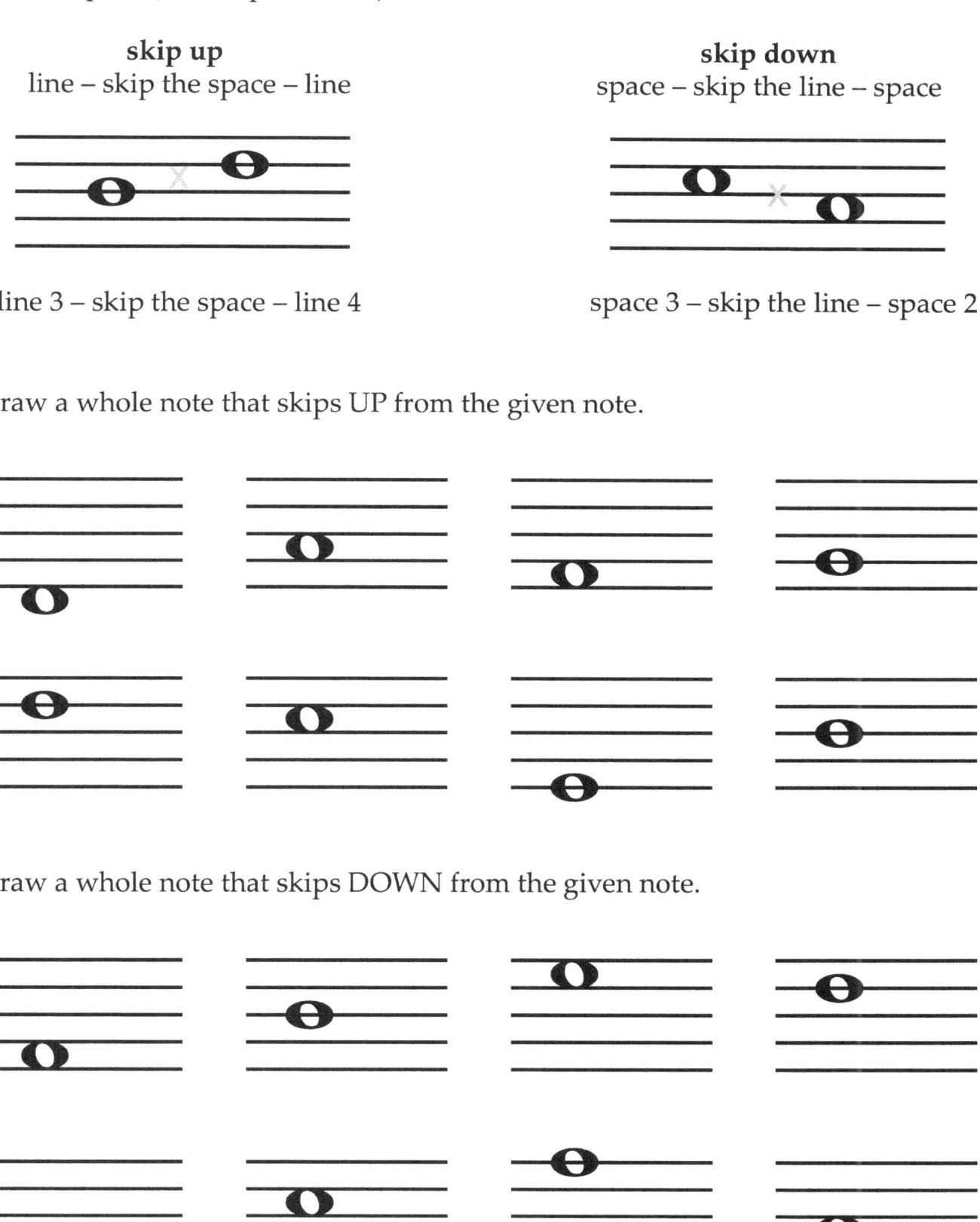

5. Ferdinand the frog wants to go to the other side of the pond to catch some flies. Write the letter on each lily pad to help Ferdinand get across the pond.

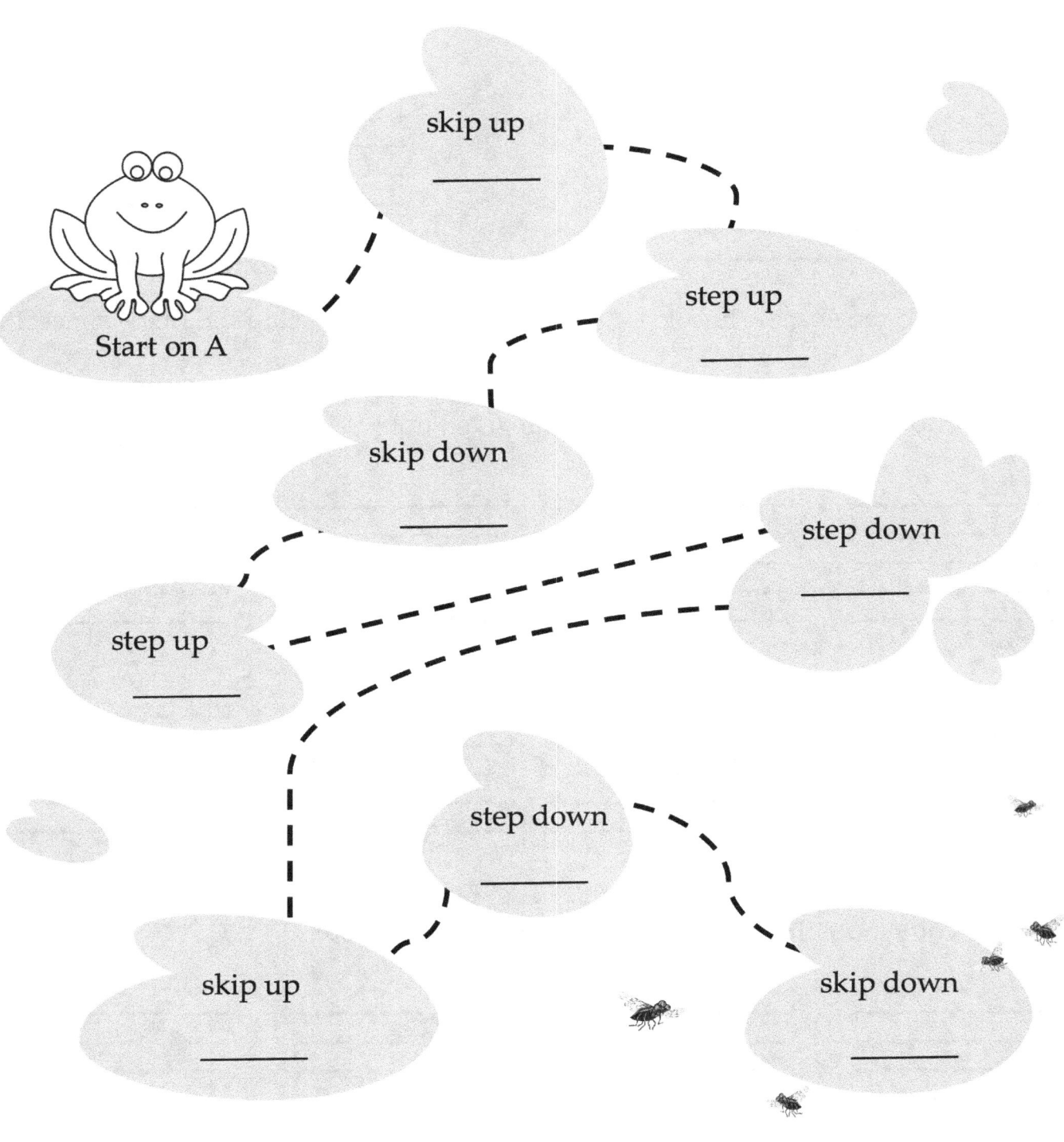

6. Use your your instrument and play the notes that Ferdinand's path takes. Listen to how steps and skips sound different.

What do you hear? #8

You will hear 3 notes. Circle whether the notes you hear are stepping or skipping.

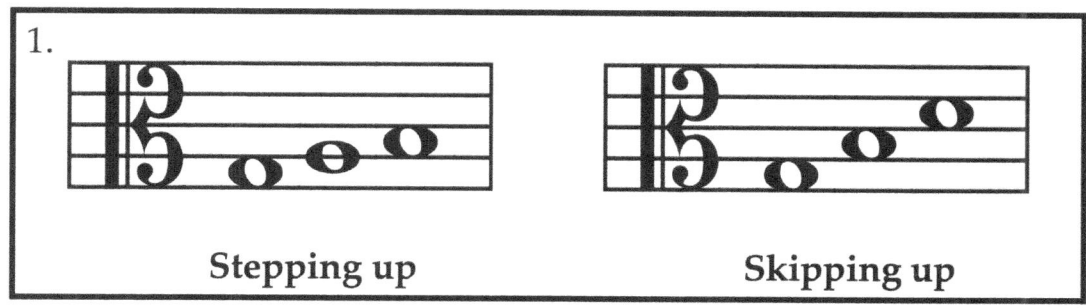

1.

Stepping up   Skipping up

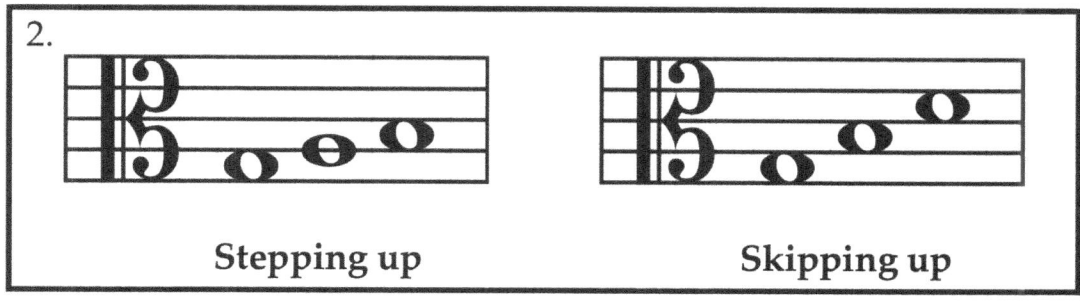

2.

Stepping up   Skipping up

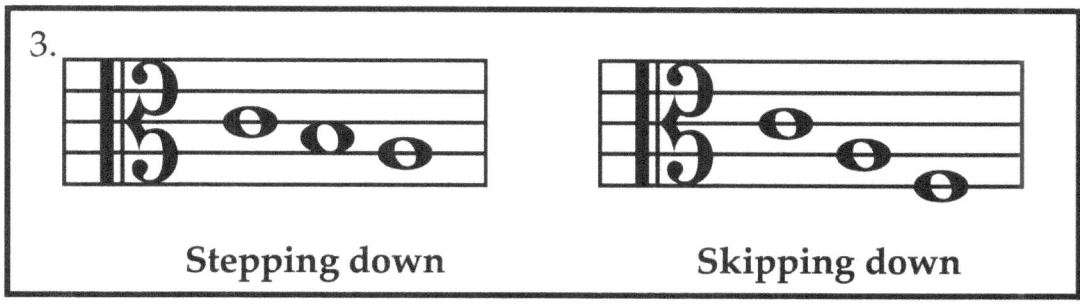

3.

Stepping down   Skipping down

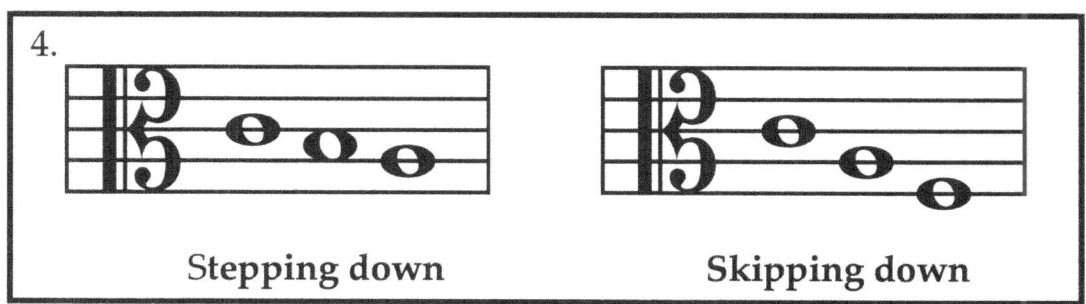

4.

Stepping down   Skipping down

*Additional ear training exercises can be found on p. 99

Choose one of the examples in each box to play.

Lesson 30

1. Draw whole notes on the staff that match the fingerboard houses. Then write the letters on the line. (Starting with the house on the C or G string, each fingerboard spells a word.)

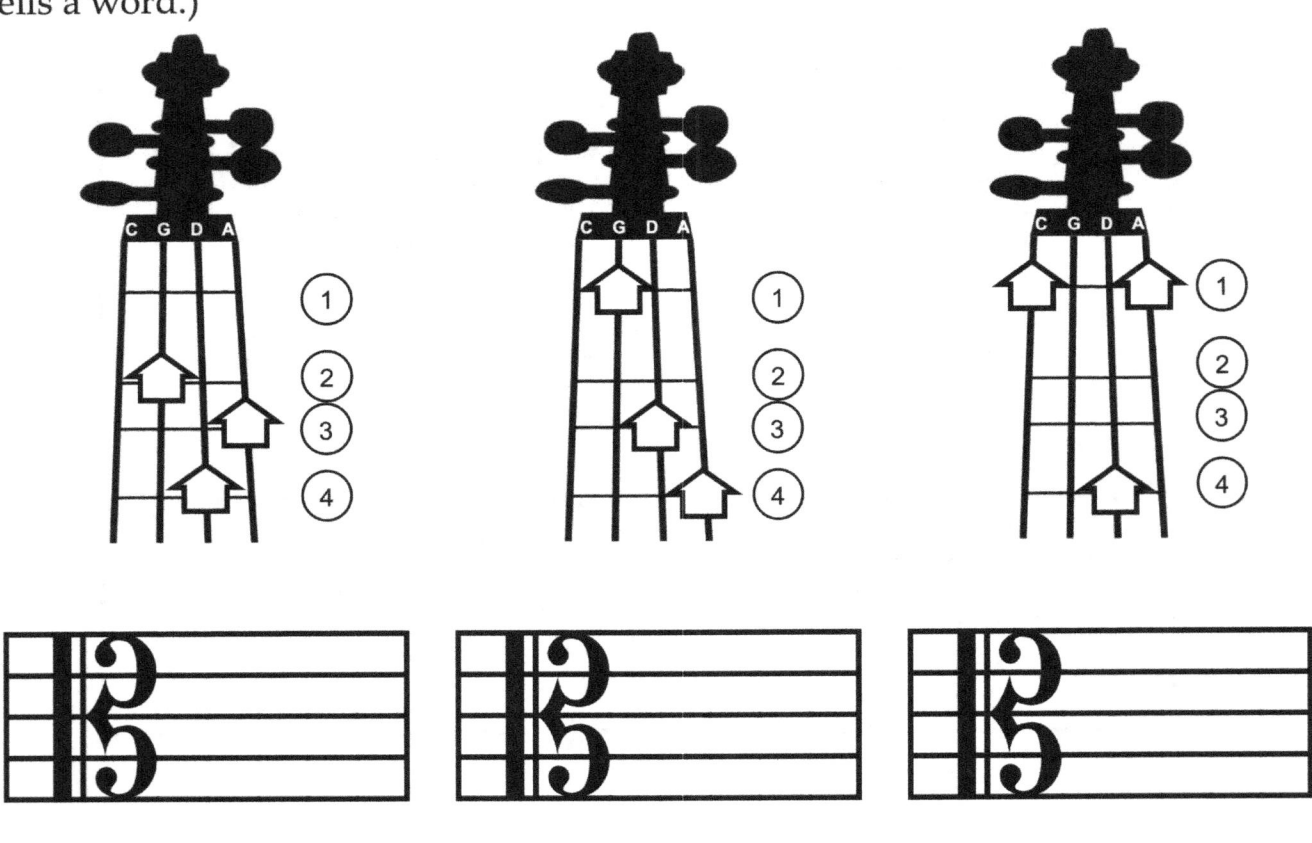

_____   _____   _____

2. Look at the example below. Write the letter in the blank that matches the term.

_____ Time Signature   _____ Bar Line   _____ Repeat Sign   _____ Dynamic

_____ Half Rest   _____ Step   _____ Skip   _____ Crescendo   _____ Diminuendo

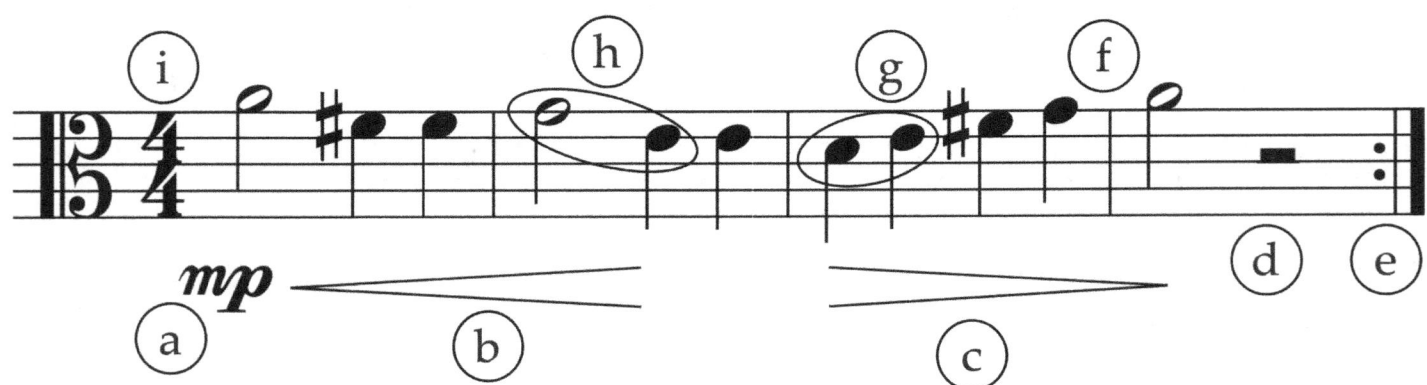

The Magic of Music Theory Book 1 - © 2025 Horsehair Music. Photocopying prohibited.

3. On the blank write the word that is on each screen.

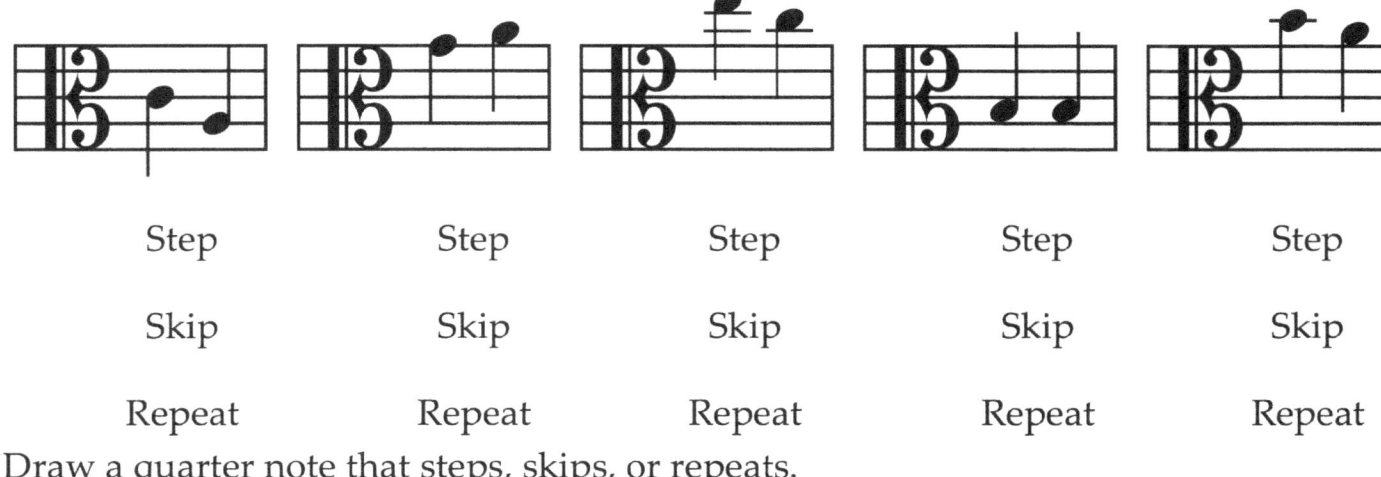

4. Circle if the notes step, skip, or repeat.

Step	Step	Step	Step	Step
Skip	Skip	Skip	Skip	Skip
Repeat	Repeat	Repeat	Repeat	Repeat

5. Draw a quarter note that steps, skips, or repeats.

| Step Up | Skip Down | Repeats | Repeats |

Lesson 31

1. Draw a line from the term to the correct part of the bow.

tip   screw   frog   grip   wrapping   ferrule   eye   stick   horsehair

Tone is sound that the viola makes when it plays. How each note starts and ends is called **articulation**. For stringed instruments, the bow does most of the articulation work. **Detaché** [day-tah-shay] means separated. This is the basic bow stroke we use to play our instrument.

⊓ This symbol means to use a **down bow**. A down bow pulls the bow from frog to toward the tip.

∨ This symbol means to use an **up bow**. An up bow pushes the bow from tip to toward the frog.

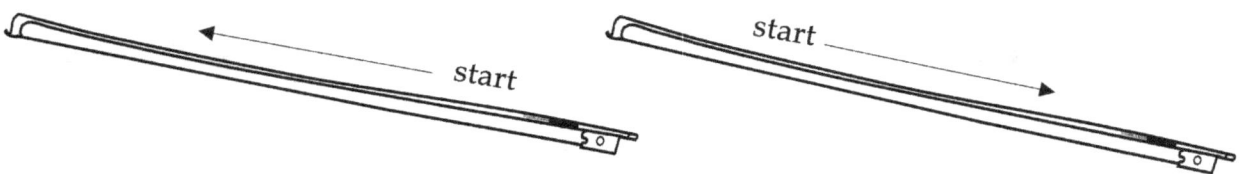

The Italian word **legato** means smooth and connected. Stringed instruments can play legato with separate bows or by playing 2 or more notes in 1 bow stroke. This is called a **slur**. A slur is marked in music by a curved line connecting the note heads. Slurs are drawn above or below the staff by the note heads opposite of the stems. If the stems are going different directions, the slur is always drawn above the staff.

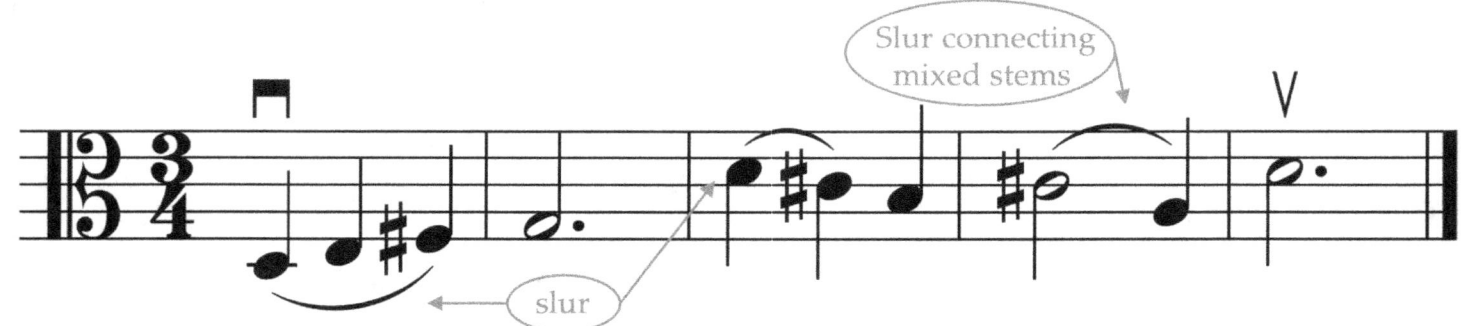

2. Draw in the slurs and bow marks to copy the example above.

The Magic of Music Theory Book 1 - © 2025 Horsehair Music. Photocopying prohibited.

Staccato means short or detached. Staccato is the opposite of legato. To play staccato we stop the bow between every note. Staccato is written in the music by placing a dot centered above or below the notehead. The dot can be placed above or below the staff or in a space on the staff.

3. Add a staccato dot to each quarter note like the example above.

 **?** *Did you know?* **Staccato dots** are different than dotted half notes! The dot for a dotted half note always goes *beside* the note head on the right side. The staccato dot goes *above* or *below* the note.

4. Draw a circle around all the staccato notes. Draw a square around all the dotted half notes.

5. Name a piece you have played that uses staccato.

_____

6. Name a piece you have played that uses legato.

_____

7. Draw the bowing symbol.
   When the bow moves from the frog toward the tip.

   When the bow moves from the tip toward the frog.

Lesson 32

Tempo means speed. The terms describing tempos are in Italian. Tempo markings are written above the first line of a piece. You will see them directly above the time signature.

Slow

⬇

Fast

Largo – very slow
Adagio – slow
Andante – a walking speed
Allegro – fast, happy with energy
Presto – very fast

1. Draw a line from the tempo marking to the vehicle it matches.

Allegro   Adagio   Andante   Largo   Presto

2. Looking at the example below. Write the letter in the blank that matches the term.

_____ Time Signature _____ Tempo _____ Staccato _____ Slur _____ Step Up

_____ Up bow _____ Down bow _____ Dynamic _____ Skip Down

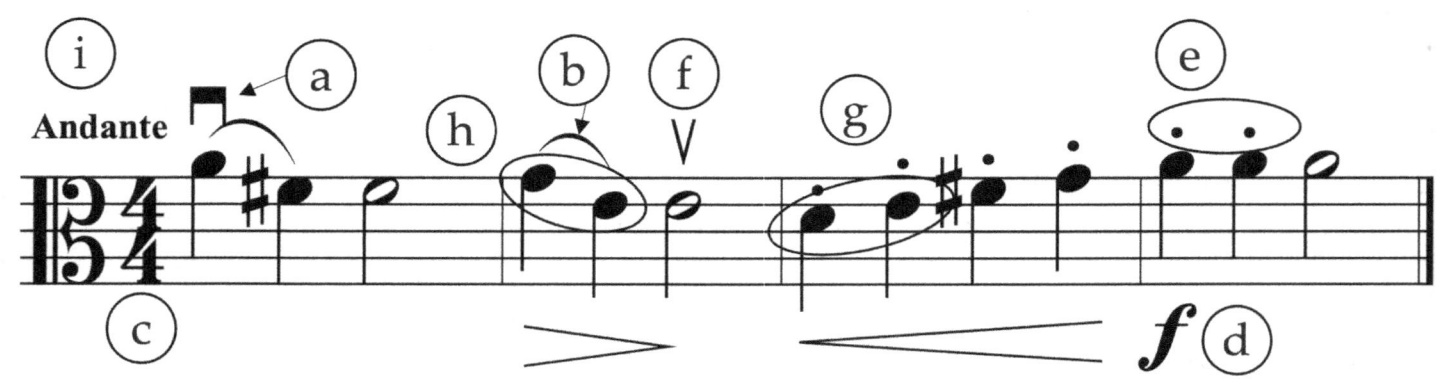

The Magic of Music Theory Book 1 - © 2025 Horsehair Music. Photocopying prohibited.

3. Write the tempo that matches the definition. (Adagio, Allegro, Andante, Largo, Presto)

Fast, happy with energy _____   Very Fast _____

Very Slow _____   Slow _____

Walking Speed _____

4. Draw the note on the staff that matches the fingerboard house. Write the letter name on the blank.

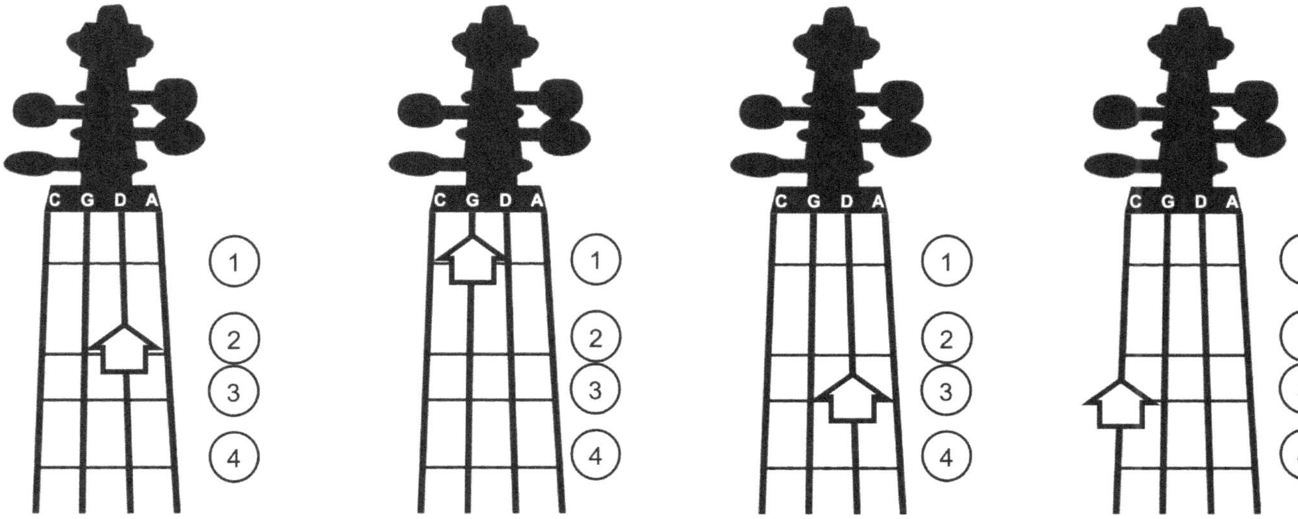

Letter: _____   _____   _____   _____

5. Draw a whole note following the directions under each staff.

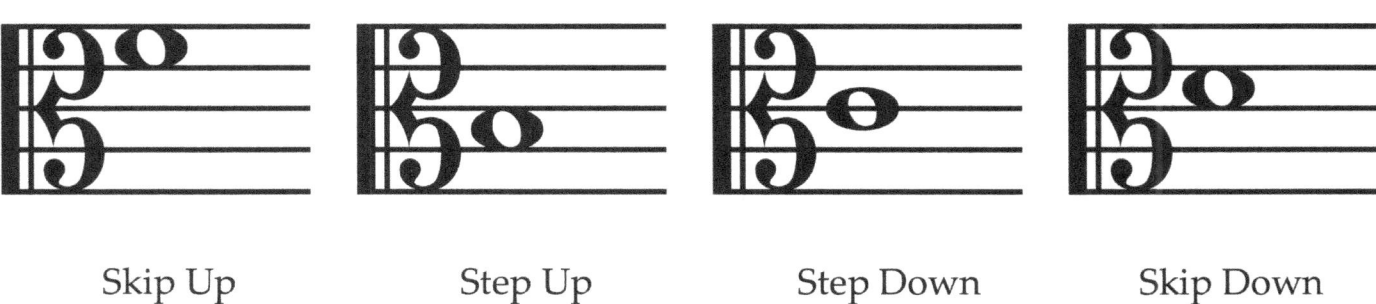

Skip Up   Step Up   Step Down   Skip Down

What do you hear? #9

You will hear an example from a classical piece. Circle whether the music you hear is Largo – very slow, Andante – walking speed, Allegro – fast, or Presto – very fast.

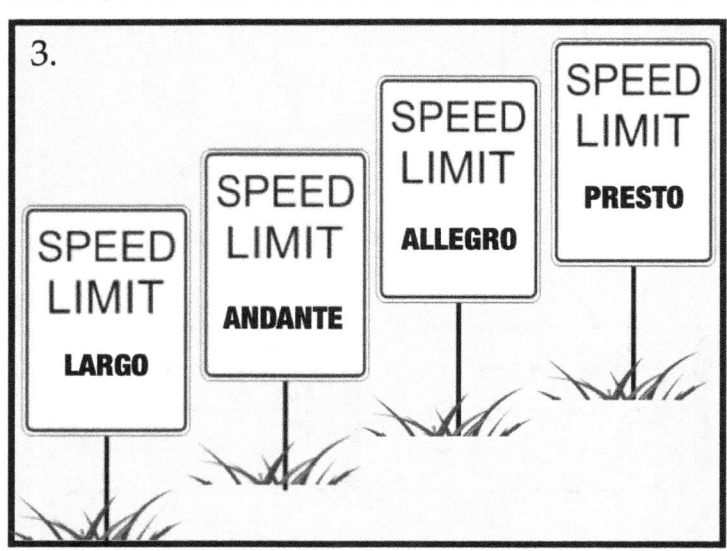

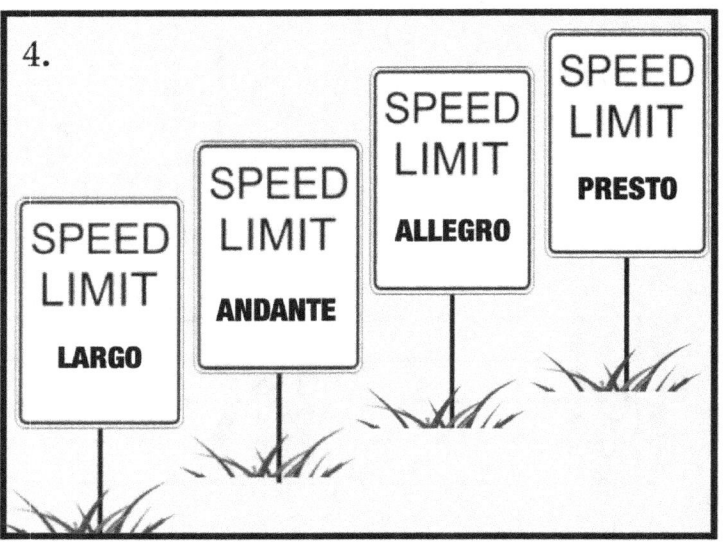

* Additional ear training exercises can be found on p. 101

The Magic of Music Theory Book 1 - © 2025 Horsehair Music. Photocopying prohibited.

The teacher should choose one example below for questions 1 - 4.

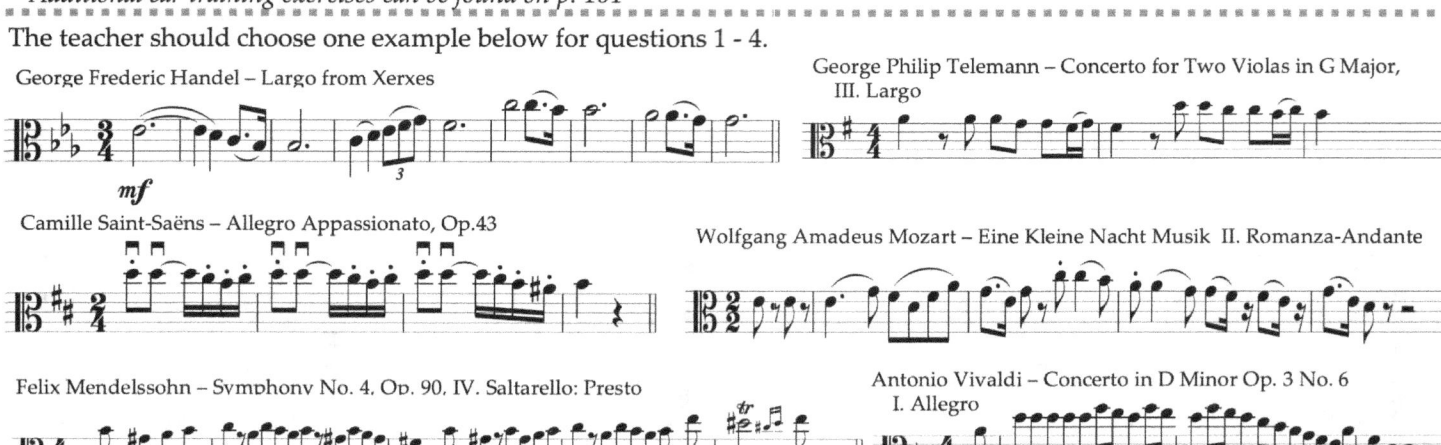

George Frederic Handel – Largo from Xerxes

George Philip Telemann – Concerto for Two Violas in G Major, III. Largo

Camille Saint-Saëns – Allegro Appassionato, Op.43

Wolfgang Amadeus Mozart – Eine Kleine Nacht Musik II. Romanza-Andante

Felix Mendelssohn – Symphony No. 4, Op. 90, IV. Saltarello: Presto

Antonio Vivaldi – Concerto in D Minor Op. 3 No. 6 I. Allegro

Lesson 33

1. Write the half step and whole step major scale pattern on the lines below.

    Begin ____ ____ ____ ____ ____ ____ ____

2. How many players are in a string quartet? _____

3. How many beats does a dotted half note receive? _____

4. How many lines does a staff have?_____

5. How many spaces does a staff have? _____

6. Draw the clefs.

    Treble Clef   Bass Clef   Alto Clef

    ═══════════   ═══════════   ═══════════
    ═══════════   ═══════════   ═══════════
    ═══════════   ═══════════   ═══════════
    ═══════════   ═══════════   ═══════════
    ═══════════   ═══════════   ═══════════

7. Match the term to the definition. (Adagio, Allegro, Andante, Largo, Presto)

    Very slow _____   Fast, with energy _____

    Very fast _____   Walking speed _____

    Slow _____

8. Find the tempo markings in the word search.

D	P	G	L	E	R	G	O	W	F
X	R	D	A	N	D	A	N	T	E
G	E	X	R	D	D	D	C	G	O
T	S	T	G	X	B	A	D	J	P
F	T	C	O	Q	F	G	A	B	I
K	O	A	R	C	O	I	D	E	Z
A	L	L	E	G	R	O	F	E	Z

9. Write in the number of beats each note or rest receives in the heart. Then write the counts for each on the blanks.

Beats:

Counts: ___ ___ ___ ___   ___   ___ ___ ___

10. Write the letter names under each note.

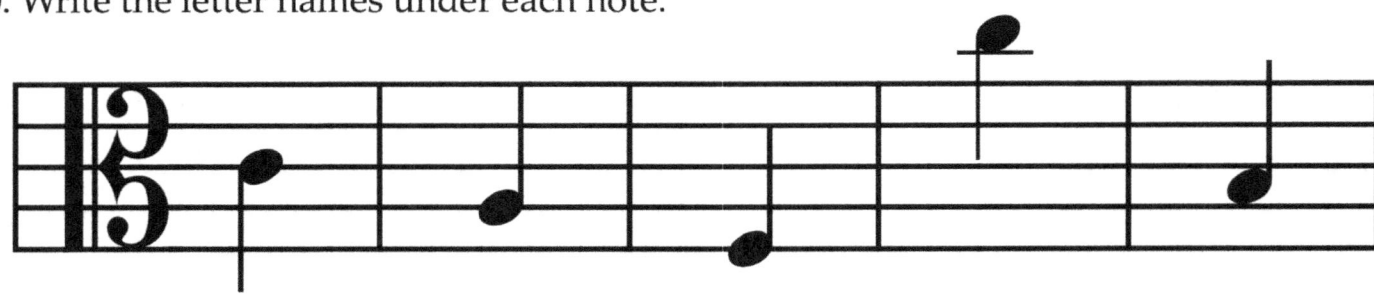

___   ___   ___   ___   ___

11. Follow the steps. After you complete each step, mark a ✅ in the box.
   ❑ Circle the symbol that raises a note a half step.
   ❑ Draw a square around the symbol that lowers a note a half step.
   ❑ Draw a triangle around the symbol showing an up bow.
   ❑ Draw a star around the symbol showing a down bow.
   ❑ Write the number of beats each note, or rest receives.
   ❑ Write the letters for each note in the houses.

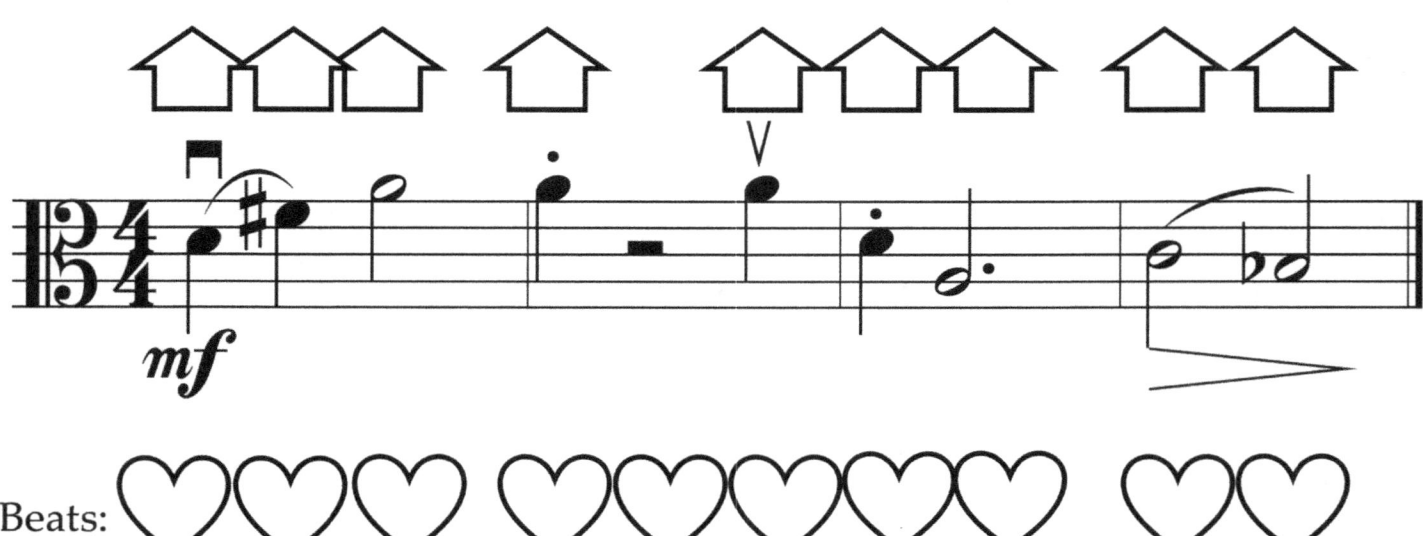

Beats:

Glossary

Adagio – [tempo mark] slow. (p. 88, 89, 91)

Allegro – [tempo mark] fast, happy with energy. (p. 88, 89, 90, 91, 101)

Alto Clef – violas read music using this clef; sometimes called the "C-clef" because the clef points to C line on the staff. (p. 23, 25, 91)

Andante – [tempo mark] walking speed. (p. 88, 89, 90, 91, 101)

Bar line – a vertical line dividing the staff into measures. (p. 59)

Bass Clef – cellos read music using this clef; sometimes called the "F-clef" because the clef points to "F" line on the staff. (p. 23, 25, 91)

Chamber Music - a small group of people play together. (p.9)

Crescendo – [dynamic sign] grow gradually louder. (p. 17, 38, 67)

Detaché – [bow stroke] separate bows. (p. 86)

Diminuendo – [dynamic sign] grow gradually softer. (p. 17, 38, 67)

Duet – two people playing together. (p. 9, 52)

Dotted Half Note – gets 3 beats in 4/4 time. (p. 12, 37, 38)

Double Bar Line – a thin line followed by a thick line; always found at the end of a piece. (p. 59)

Down Bow – moving the bow from frog toward the tip. (p. 86)

Eighth Note – two eighth notes share 1 beat; each eighth note gets "½" a beat in 4/4 time. (p. 68)

Forte – [dynamic sign] Italian word meaning loud. (p. 17)

Frequency – the number of sound waves occurring in one second of time. (p. 38)

Half Note – gets 2 beats in 4/4 time. (p. 12, 42, 43)

Half Rest – rest for 2 beats in 4/4 time; looks like a hat. (Tip: *H*at and *H*alf both start with "H.") (p. 13, 20, 42, 43)

Half Step – closest distance between two notes; fingers are close together on the fingerboard. (p. 54)

Keynote – first note of a scale; also called the tonic. (p. 73, 75)

Largo – [tempo mark] very slow. (p. p. 88, 89, 90, 91, 101)

Ledger Line – a small line that extends the staff; it can be above or below the 5 staff lines. (p. 29)

Legato – smooth and connected; marked with a slur. (p. 86)

Luthier – a person who makes or repairs stringed instruments. (p. 57)

Measure – the section on the staff between bar lines. (p. 59)

Mezzo Forte – [dynamic sign] medium loud; softer than forte, but louder than mezzo piano. (p. 17, 67)

Mezzo Piano – [dynamic sign] medium soft; louder than piano, but softer than mezzo forte. (p. 17, 67)

Music Alphabet – first seven letters of the English alphabet. (p. 7, 21, 22, 27, 51, 77)

Note Head – the round part of the note. (p. 12, 15)

Open String – playing a string with no fingers on the fingerboard. (p. 10, 18)

Piano – [dynamic sign] Italian word meaning soft. (p. 17, 38)

Presto – [tempo marking] very fast (p. 88, 89, 90, 91, 101)

Quarter Note – gets 1 beat in 4/4 time. (p. 12, 31, 32)

Quarter Rest – rest for 1 beat in 4/4 time. (p. 13, 20)

Repeat Sign – two dots in front of a double bar line; ply that section again. (p. 59, 84)

Rest – musical symbol for silence; stop playing. (p. 13)

Rhythm – how long or short we hold a pitch. (p. 12)

Scale – 8 consecutive notes in a whole step and half step pattern. (p. 70, 75)

Skip – skip a finger on the fingerboard; skip a letter in the music alphabet; skip a line or a space on the staff; A skip on the staff is line note to line note or space note to space note. (p. 77, 80, 81, 83)

Slur – a curved line that starts and ends just above or below the notehead; means to play legato and all notes on 1 bow stroke. (p. 86)

Staccato – play short or detached; marked with a dot above or below the note head. (p. 87)

Staff – 5 lines and 4 spaces. (p. 15)

Step – the letter before or after a letter in the music alphabet; the line or space above or below a note on the staff; the finger number before or after a finger on the fingerboard. (p. 51, 53, 54, 55, 83)

String Quartet – four people playing together; most often 2 violins, 1 viola and 1 cello. (p. 9)

Tempo – speed; how fast or slow music is played. (p. 88)

Time Signature – found at the beginning of a piece; top number tells the number of beats in each measure; the bottom number tells what kind of note gets 1 beat; when 4 is on the bottom, it means the quarter note gets one beat. (p. 59)

Tonic – first note of a scale; sometimes also called the keynote. (p. 73)

Treble Clef – violins read music using this clef; sometimes called the "G-clef" because the clef points to G line on the staff. (p. 23, 24)

Trio – three people playing together. (p. 9)

Up Bow – moving the bow from the tip toward the frog. (p. 86)

Whole Note – gets 4 beats in 4/4 time. (p. 12)

Whole Rest – rest for 4 beats in 4/4 time, or rest for the whole measure. (p. 13, 20)

Whole Step – 2 half steps together; space between fingers on the fingerboard. (p. 54)

Composer Index

Note Drill

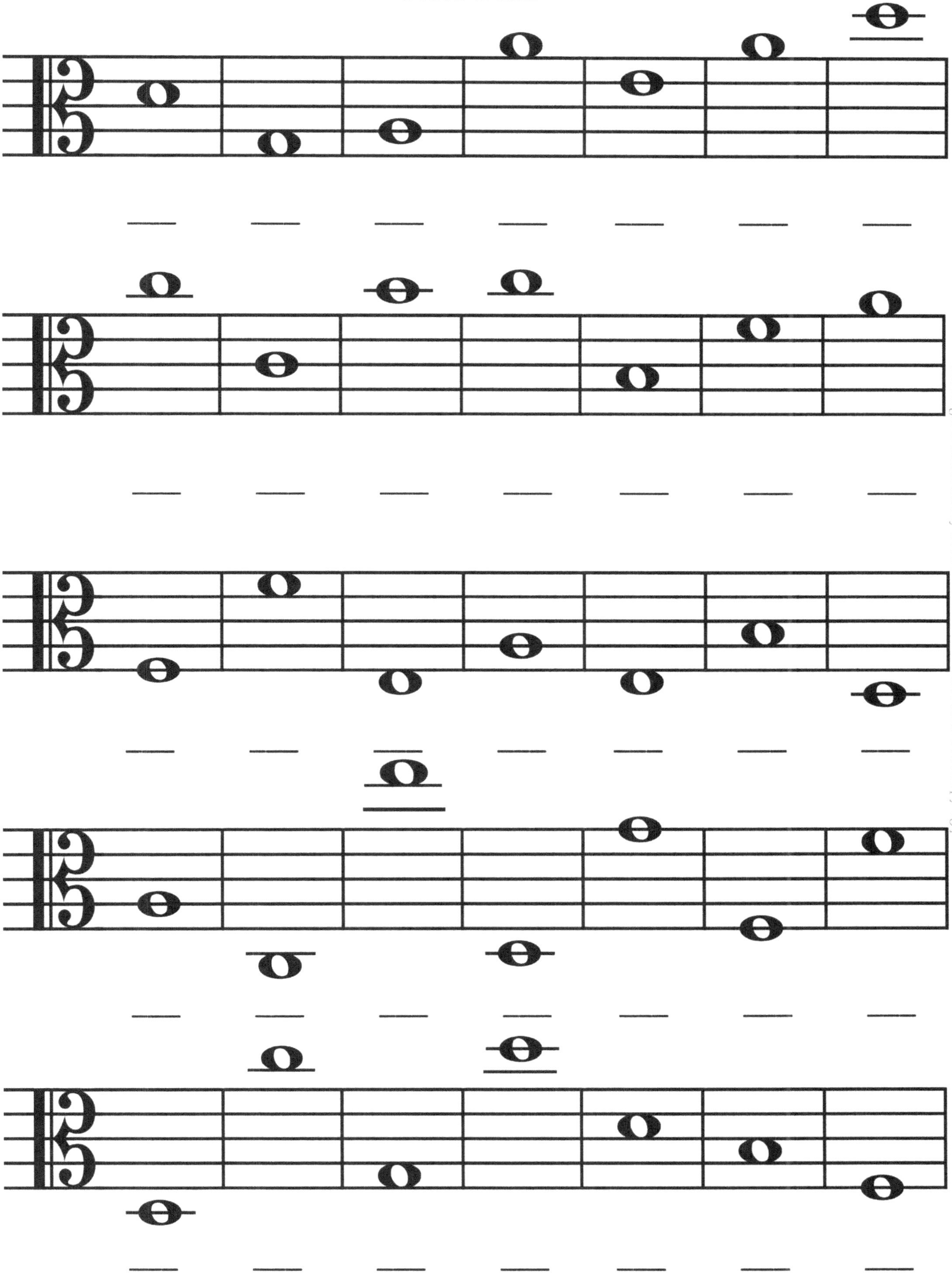

The Magic of Music Theory Book 1 - © 2025 Horsehair Music. Photocopying prohibited.

Extra Ear Training Practice A: Open Strings

Color the house of the string that you hear.

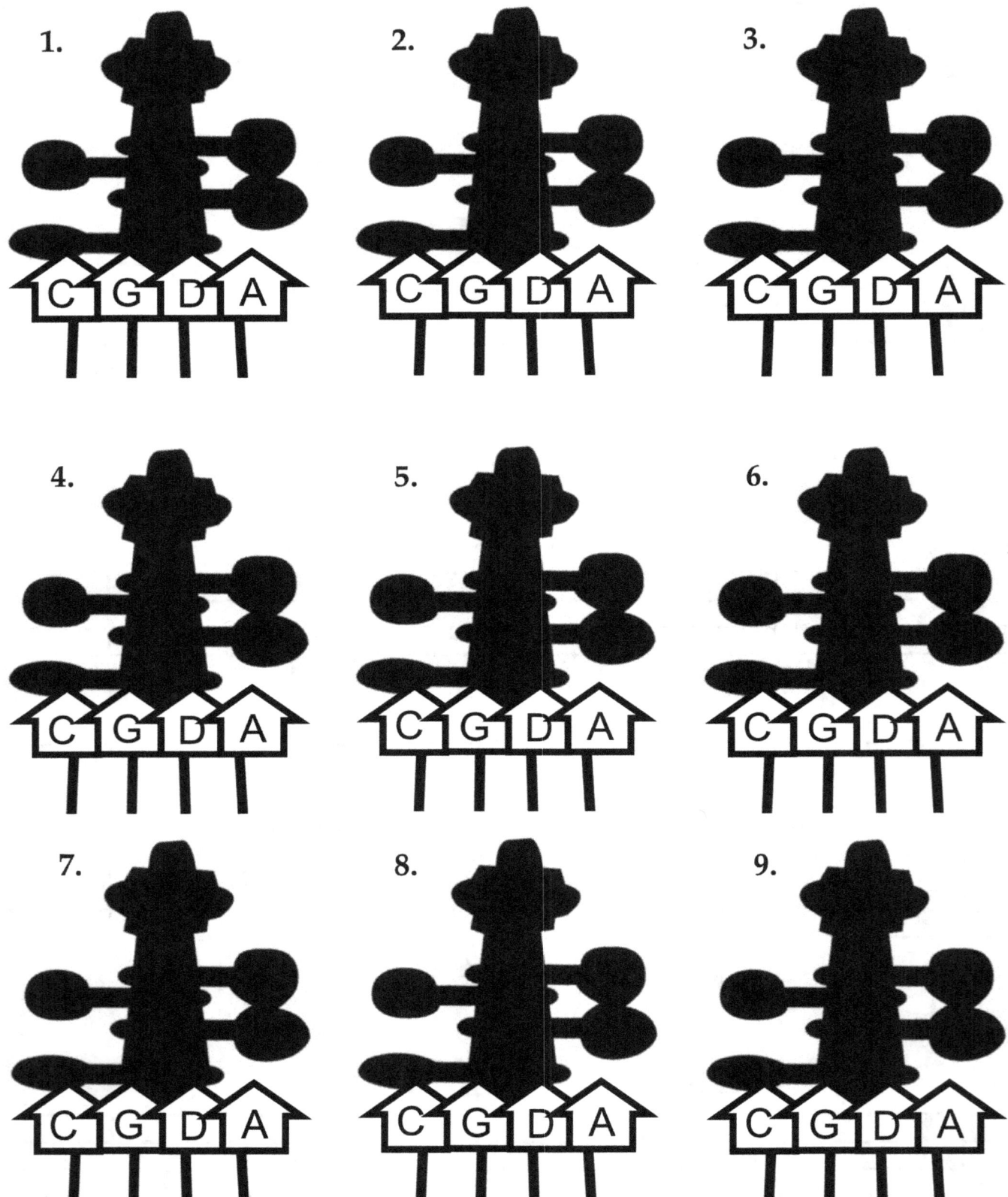

Choose a rhythm pattern to play on an open string.

Extra Ear Training Practice B: Dynamics

Circle the dynamic you hear.

1	2	3
f *mf* *p*	*f* *mf* *p*	*f* *mf* *p*

4	5	6
f *mf* *p*	*f* *mf* *p*	*f* *mf* *p*

Circle if you hear a crescendo, getting louder, or diminuendo, getting softer.

7	8	9
crescendo *diminuendo*	*crescendo* *diminuendo*	*crescendo* *diminuendo*

10	11	12
crescendo *diminuendo*	*crescendo* *diminuendo*	*crescendo* *diminuendo*

Choose one example for questions 1 – 6 and play with an exaggerated dynamic.

Johann Sebastian Bach – March

Ludwig van Beethoven – Symphony No. 5
I. Allegro con brio

Franz Joseph Haydn – "Surprise" Symphony
II. Andante

For questions 7-12, choose an example or create your own example and exaggerate the dynamics.

Luigi Boccherini – Minuet

Wolfgang Amadeus Mozart – Requiem
Lacrimosa

Johann Sebastian Bach – Brandenburg Concerto No 5
I. Allegro

Extra Ear Training Practice C: Stepping Up, Down or Repeating

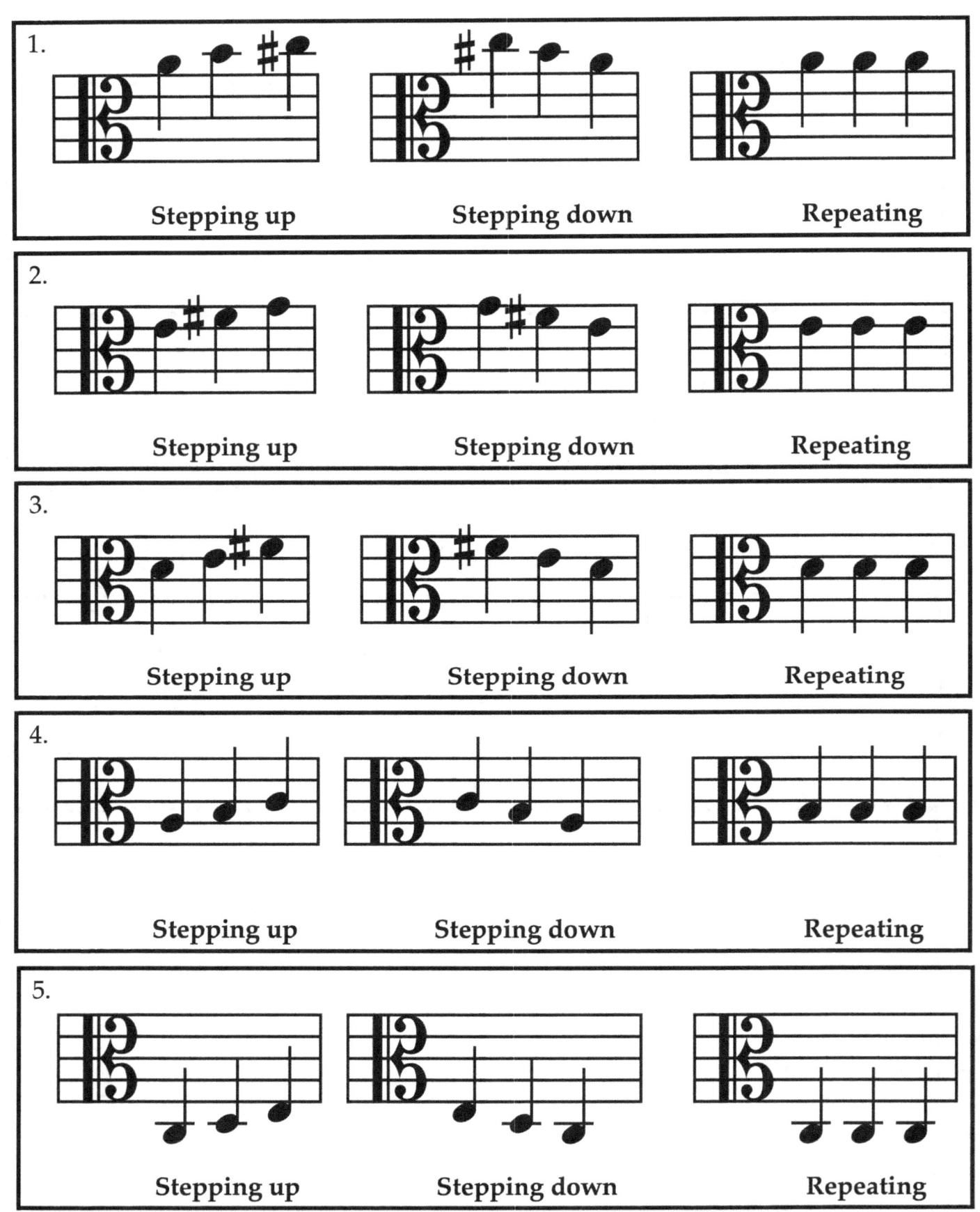

Choose one of the examples in each box to play.

Extra Ear Training Practice D: Stepping or Skipping

Circle if the notes you hear skip or step.

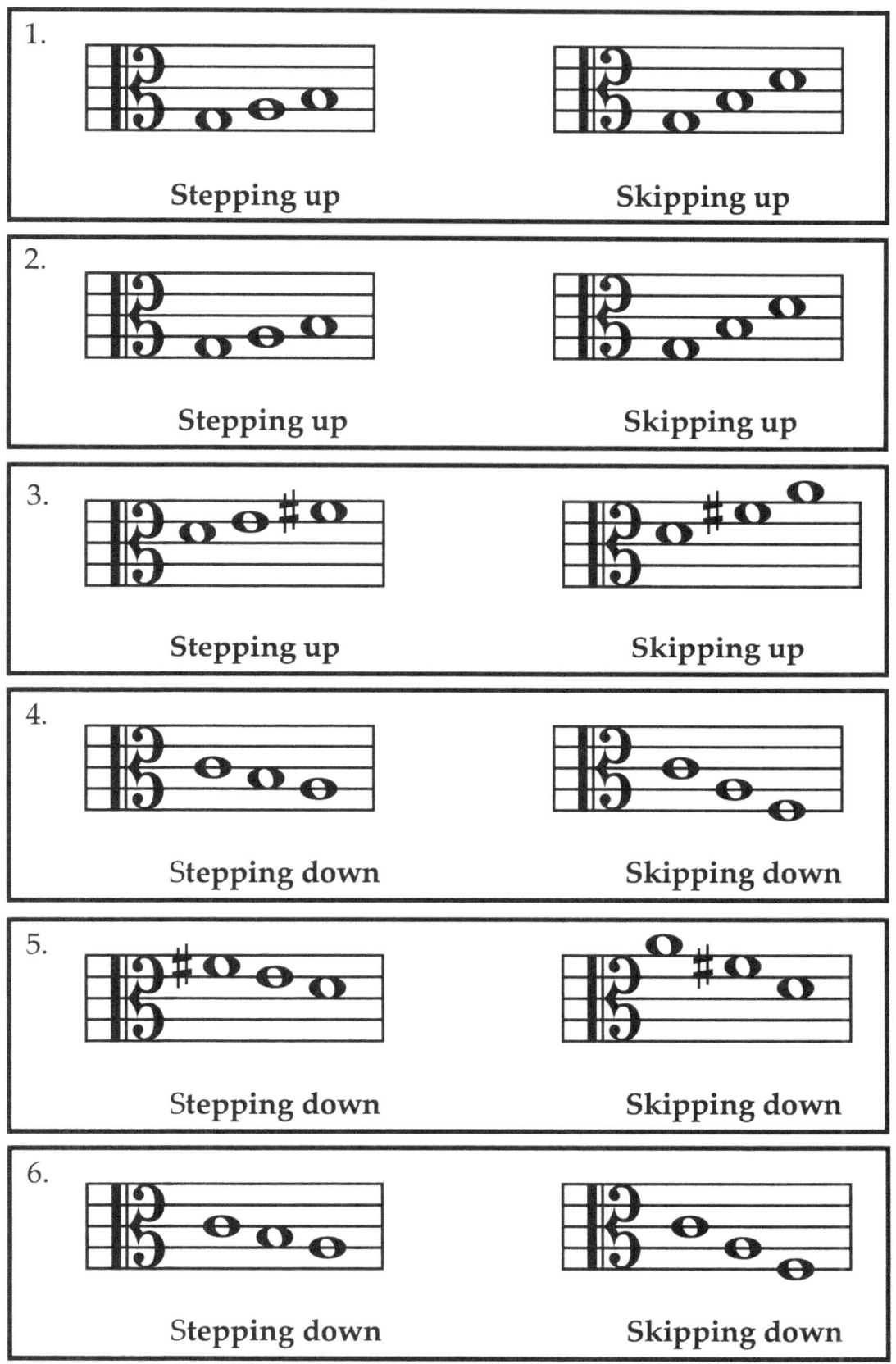

1.

Stepping up   Skipping up

2.

Stepping up   Skipping up

3.

Stepping up   Skipping up

4.

Stepping down   Skipping down

5.

Stepping down   Skipping down

6.

Stepping down   Skipping down

Choose one example from each box.

Extra Ear Training Practice E: Rhythm ID

Circle the rhythm pattern you hear in each box.

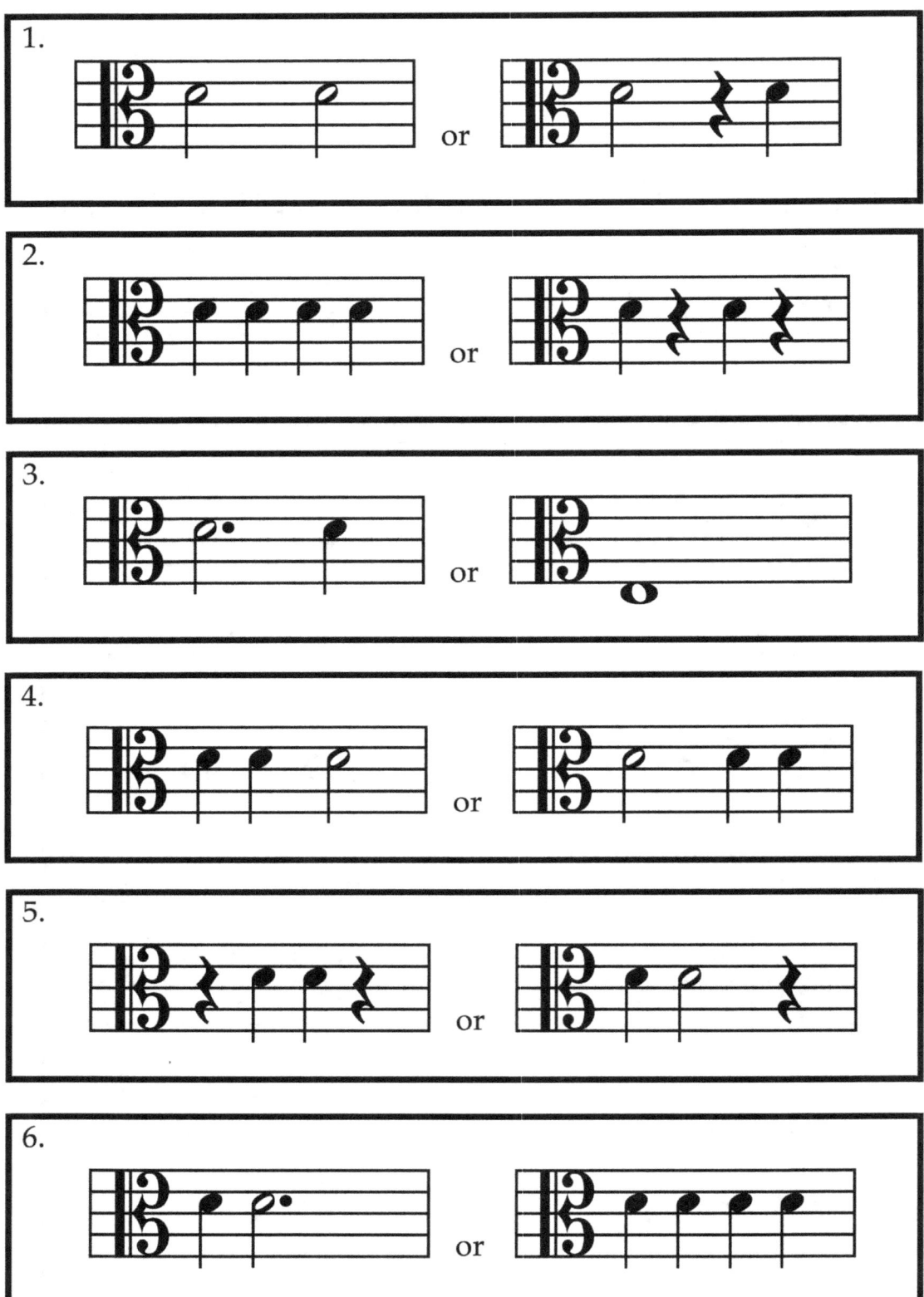

The Magic of Music Theory Book 1 - © 2025 Horsehair Music. Photocopying prohibited.

Extra Ear Training Practice F: Tempo

Remember, tempo means speed. You will hear an example from a classical piece. Circle whether the music you hear is Largo – very slow, Andante – walking speed, Allegro – fast, or Presto – very fast.

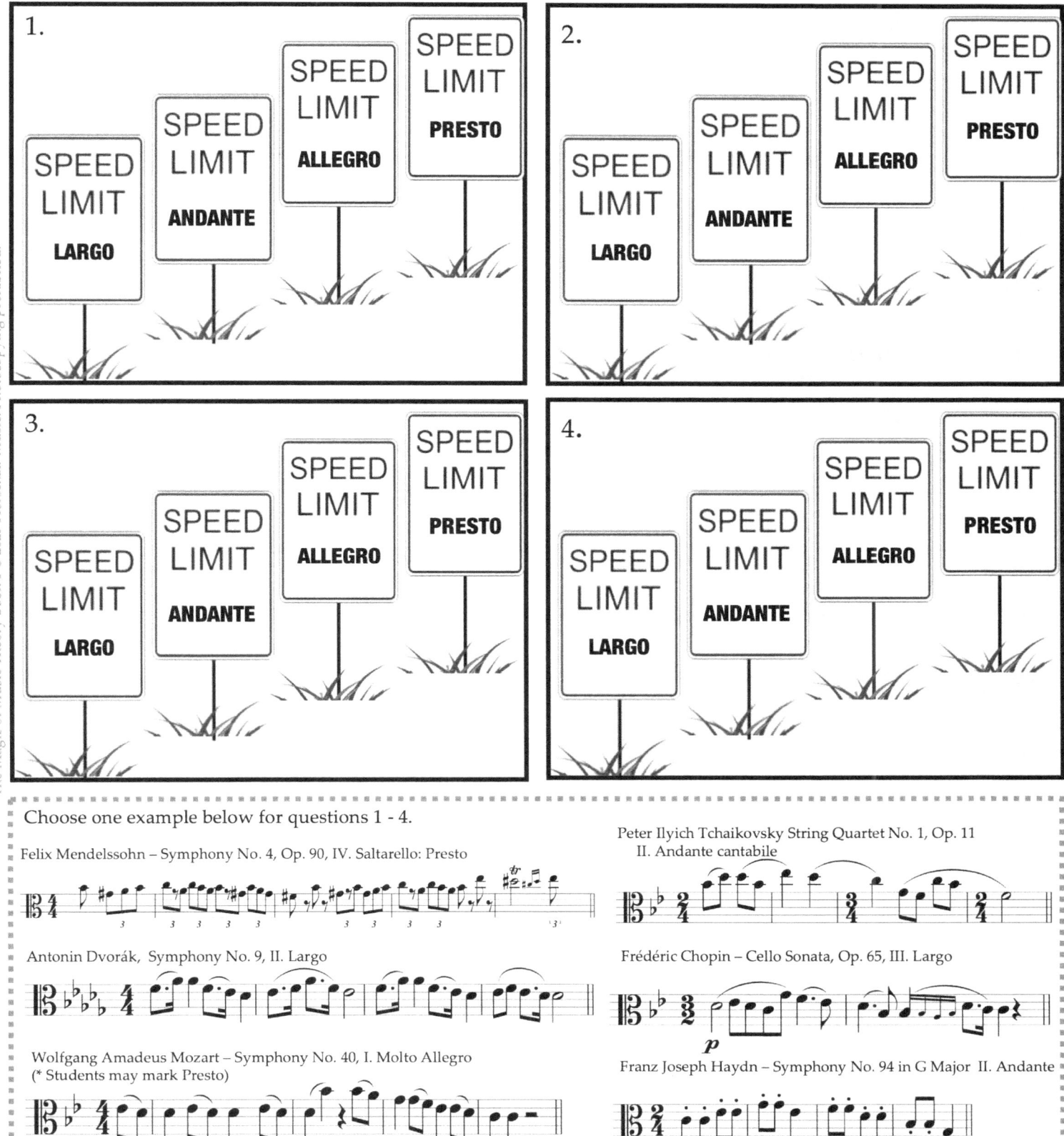

Choose one example below for questions 1 - 4.

Felix Mendelssohn – Symphony No. 4, Op. 90, IV. Saltarello: Presto

Antonin Dvorák, Symphony No. 9, II. Largo

Wolfgang Amadeus Mozart – Symphony No. 40, I. Molto Allegro
(* Students may mark Presto)

Peter Ilyich Tchaikovsky String Quartet No. 1, Op. 11
   II. Andante cantabile

Frédéric Chopin – Cello Sonata, Op. 65, III. Largo

Franz Joseph Haydn – Symphony No. 94 in G Major II. Andante

Hooray!

_____

has completed
The Magic of Music Theory
Book 1
and is now ready for Book 2

_____

(Teacher)

_____

(Date)

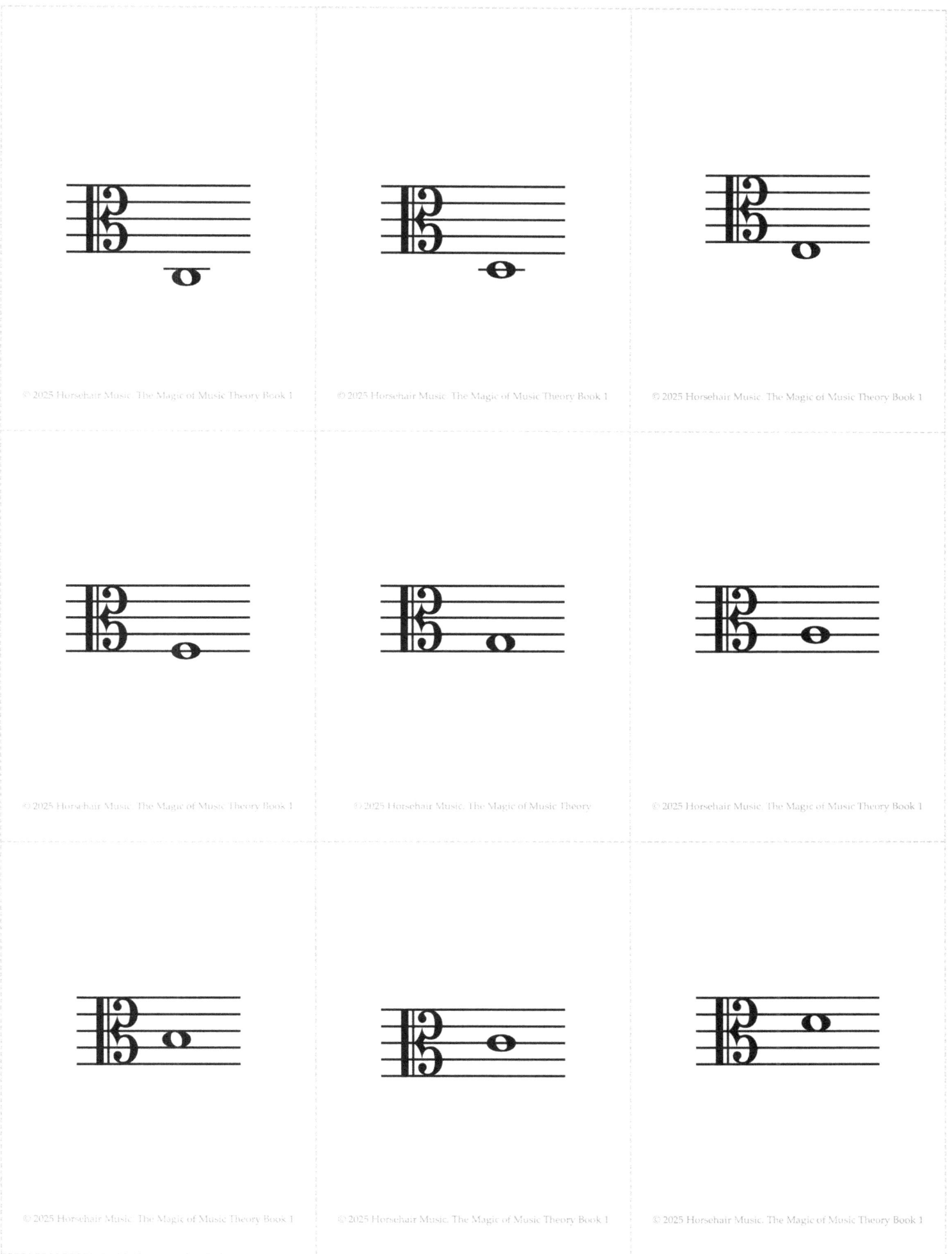

E

2nd finger on C

D

1st finger on C

C

Open C

A

1st finger on G

G

Open G
or
4th finger on C

F

3rd finger on C

D

Open D
or
4th finger on G

C

3rd finger on G

B

2nd finger on G

mf

mezzo forte

Dynamic –
medium loud

mezzo piano

Dynamic –
medium soft

Repeat Sign

Ledger Line

Diminuendo

Gradually
growing softer

Crescendo

Gradually
growing louder

Slur

Legato –
smooth and
connected

Staccato

Short, detached

2 eighth notes

Share 1 beat

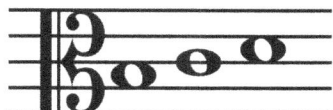

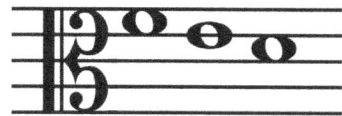

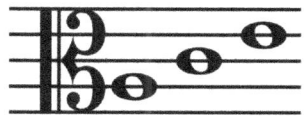

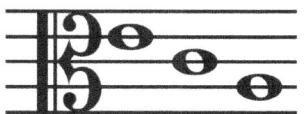

Largo

Presto

Tonic
or
Keynote

Half Step

Whole Step

Skip Up

Step Down

Step Up

Very Fast

Very Slow

Skip Down

Whole Step

2 half steps together.

Space between fingers.

Half Step

The smallest distance between two notes.

Fingers close together

First Note of the Scale